ART OF AUSTRALIA

AUSTRALIA

1788-1941

AN EXHIBITION OF AUSTRALIAN ART
HELD IN THE UNITED STATES OF AMERICA
AND THE DOMINION OF CANADA
UNDER THE AUSPICES OF THE
CARNEGIE CORPORATION

COMPILED AND EDITED BY SYDNEY URE SMITH, O.B.E.
SYDNEY, AUSTRALIA

NEW YORK
PUBLISHED FOR THE CARNEGIE CORPORATION
BY THE MUSEUM OF MODERN ART
1941

408074

Selection Committee for the Exhibition

CHAIRMAN:

WILL ASHTON, O.B.E., *Director, National Art Gallery, N.S.W.*

COMMITTEE MEMBERS:

Professor H. C. RICHARDS, *Representative, Carnegie Corporation in Australia*

R. J. F. BOYER, *Representing the Government of the Commonwealth of Australia*

J. S. MacDONALD, *Director, National Art Gallery of Victoria*

G. V. F. MANN, C.B.E., *Chairman, Commonwealth Art Advisory Board*

LOUIS McCUBBIN, *Director, National Art Gallery of South Australia*

SYDNEY URE SMITH, O.B.E., *President, Society of Artists, Vice-President, Australian Academy of Art*

ADVISORY MEMBER TO THE COMMITTEE:

Professor THEODORE SIZER, *Director, Yale University Art Gallery, U.S.A.*

Acknowledgments

THE Committee desire to acknowledge their grateful thanks to the following institutions and people for their assistance in connection with the loan of works of art for the exhibition.

The Trustees of the National Gallery of Victoria, The Trustees of the National Museum, Melbourne, The Trustees of the National Art Gallery of New South Wales, The Trustees of the National Gallery of South Australia, The Trustees of the Queensland National Art Gallery, The Trustees of the Public Library, Museum and Art Gallery of Western Australia, The Trustees of the Tasmanian Museum and Art Gallery (Hobart), The Trustees of the Public Library of New South Wales for the Dixson Collection, The Trustees of the Warrnambool Art Gallery, Victoria, and Sir Marcus Clark, K.B.E., Mr. J. R. McGregor, Dr. R. S. Godsall, Mr. Charles Lloyd Jones, Mr. R. R. Dangar, Lieut. C. H. Rowan, A.I.F., Dr. R. M. Crookston, Mr. W. G. Buckle, Mr. S. Ure Smith, the artists who lent their work, the Yale University Art Gallery and the Australian Legation, Washington, D.C.

Foreword

THIS exhibition seeks to tell the story of Australia, not as seen by the on-looker of today, but as seen by the people themselves at each stage of the century and a half of their growth.

Perhaps no two peoples have such similar origins, such parallel conditions of growth and development, as have Australia and the United States. Their pioneers were sturdy folk of much the same stock, who looked with faith toward new lands and a life free from the restraints of the old world. They faced the challenge of a new world, with its demands for ceaseless effort, and found themselves repaid by rapidly expanding possibilities.

For a hundred years Australia went through stages of hardship, lawlessness and heroism similar to those that characterized the same period in American history. There were no warlike tribes like the North American Indians to contend with; but the taming of a vast continent where heat and drought, fire and flood succeeded each other in a way calculated to test the strongest spirit, called for endurance and courage equal to that of any of the pioneers of history.

Against the background of the bark paintings left by the world's most primitive aborigines, the art in the present exhibition records the progress of European, and particularly British, people in this struggle.

A tenacious conservatism has until recently dominated the artistic scene in Australia. This is largely due to the relatively short time that the white man has lived there, and to his natural nostalgia for the remembered old world. It has taken Australia a long time to absorb and digest her own unique surroundings, to put the new overseas movements in art into a proper perspective, and to weld them into an artistic idiom of her own.

The material is there in plenty: the strange and rather grim beauty of her landscape, and the very individual life of her people, in whom the love of independence and of fearless experiment persists.

Throughout this exhibition one can detect the pungent flavour of the Australian bush, something of the colour and vitality that distinguish the Australian in other fields.

If the art of a nation is to flourish, her painters must have protection and encouragement. This the United States has for some time appreciated, and has now laid the basis for a proud national art. It is hoped that Australia may some

5

day contrive to do the same for her young painters, so that the already strong foundations of her painting may be worthily built upon. This will doubtless happen when she emerges from the shadow that now lies over most of the countries of the world, and when her feet are once more set upon the way of peace.

R. G. CASEY

Australian Minister to the United States

Preface

THIS is the first comprehensive exhibition of Australian art to be sent to the United States and Canada. It represents at least one hundred and fifty years of creative effort, from painting done before the coming of the white man down to the work of young contemporaries, some of whom have been influenced by the rediscovered art of the aborigines.

The idea of a trans-Pacific exhibition was conceived by the Commonwealth Government, which appointed a Committee of Selection to assemble the material. Professor Theodore Sizer, Director of the Yale University Art Gallery, journeyed to Australia at the invitation of the Australian and New Zealand Museums and Art Galleries Association, under the auspices of the Carnegie Corporation, to advise the Committee as to the kind of work most likely to interest the American public. The cost of assembling the exhibition and shipping it to Washington has been underwritten by the Commonwealth Government; expenses in America, other than transportation, are being borne by the Carnegie Corporation. The Museum of Modern Art is circulating the exhibition in the United States and the National Gallery of Canada is arranging the tour in that Dominion.

The opening exhibitions are to be held in the National Gallery of Art, Washington, at the National Gallery of Canada, Ottawa, and at the Metropolitan Museum of Art, New York.

Thanks are due to the Right Honourable R. G. Menzies, Prime Minister of Australia, to the Honourable H. S. Foll, Minister of Information, to the Right Honourable R. G. Casey, Australian Minister in Washington, and Mrs. Casey, to R. J. F. Boyer of the American Division of the Department of Information at Sydney, to Sir Keith Murdoch of Melbourne and Charles Lloyd Jones of Sydney, to Professor H. C. Richards of Brisbane, President of the Australian and New Zealand Museums and Art Galleries Association, and to the members of the Committee of Selection who gave so generously of their time.

In the United States and Canada, to David E. Finley, Macgill James and John Walker III of the National Gallery of Art, Washington, H. O. McCurry, Director of the National Gallery of Canada, Francis Henry Taylor, Horace H. F. Jayne and Harry B. Wehle of the Metropolitan Museum of Art, Alfred H. Barr, Jr., Monroe Wheeler and Miss Elodie Courter of the Museum of Modern Art, and Wayland Williams of New Haven, who edited this catalogue.

And finally, to Will Ashton, O.B.E., Director of the National Art Gallery of New South Wales, who, as Chairman of the Committee of Selection, assured the success of the enterprise, and to Theodore Sizer of the Yale Gallery, who not only helped with the selection but was largely responsible for the myriad details of administration attendant upon the arrival of the exhibition in this country.

FREDERICK P. KEPPEL

President, Carnegie Corporation

September 1, 1941

THIS AUSTRALIA*

BY MARJORIE BARNARD

I.

DROP SCENE

AUSTRALIA, the Terra Incognita of the old world, the last continent to be discovered, is a study in variety and sameness. It has a hot, barren core, ridge after ridge of red sand, a desert of stones without water, without verdure, then sand again. This is surrounded by lands of every degree of goodness and badness, yielding almost every product and encircled by a littoral of amazing diversity, ranging from the rich lands of the northeast coast to the barren shores of the Bight open to the winds of the Pole, to the pearling grounds of the Nor' West and the unexploited Northern Territory. It is so easy to lose its unity in its infinite diversity, but it is there. Australia is a whole. It has a thousand divergences within itself but it is not like anywhere else in the world. It is a continent compacted and made strange by separation from the rest of the world for untold time, an island that has evolved by itself and grown old before the coming of the white man. It was the continent in which man had been unsuccessful. There were inhabitants—scattered tribes of black men who scarcely progressed beyond mere existence. Scientific opinion is coming more and more to see in the aboriginals a run-down and defeated people—not defeated by a superior civilization as the red Indians of North America were—but by the continent itself before the advent of the white man. They are known to be an ancient race, yet they never learned to till the soil, never progressed. There are vestiges in their language and in their tribal customs of higher race memories. Their very bodies present a riddle to which one answer is that they were once a white people, blackened through centuries by the sun, worn down by an overwhelming struggle for existence, a people defeated in the evolutionary cycle.

The continent that had rejected man grew old alone. For centuries nothing was known of it but the coast line and that imperfectly. Navigators had given

Condensed and rewritten by the author from The Home Annual, *by permission John Fairfax & Sons Pty. Ltd.*

the sandy west coast a bad name. Of the east less was known. Tasman had dredged from the darkness the wild and rocky east coast of the island which now bears his name. It was not until 1770 that Captain Cook officially discovered Australia and sailed up the east coast charting it. Coming in from the sea Botany Bay had seemed good to him. Sir Joseph Banks, who sailed with him, found it interesting country, but the "barrenest" he had ever seen. Time and distance were to soften that verdict. In 1788, in the broad daylight of the eighteenth century, a thousand men came to settle this unknown continent. Their destination was Botany Bay, for that was the only point on the whole east coast of which they had any favourable report. Within a few miles of the Bay they had the good luck to find "the finest harbour in the world, in which a thousand sail of the line may ride in the most perfect security." There in a little cove, thickly wooded, with deep water for the ships, a run of fresh water, they landed and began slowly, with infinite hardship, to make their way in the new world.

It was a new world unlike anything else white men had known. They found an old coast, brown headland after brown headland, worn down to their ultimate resistance by sea and wind, with scallops of shining sand between them where the long Pacific rollers broke in perpetual surf. Just beyond the sea-bitten rim of the coast the bush began and stretched as far as their eyes or imagination could go. It was as monotonous as the sea, as silent as the sky, and all through the year it was the same, evergreen. The trees were infinite variations of one tree, the eucalypt, their trunks shaggy or smooth, the narrow restless leaves edge on to the sun, conserving the precious water their roots sucked deep down in the pale dry soil. Between them grew sparse undergrowth, woody and spiny, showing a richer, darker green in the gullies beside the water holes. It was a land of little water, of lovely distances, bloomed grape-blue, of high blue skies, of strange flowers, of brilliant sunshine, dry light, dry earth, dry air, with the aromatic taste of the bush. The birds and animals were strange, the mopoke for the nightingale, the kangaroo for the deer, the koala for the squirrel, the only familiar thing perhaps a crow, cawing in a hollow world. Above all there was nothing for the hungry voyagers to eat. The new world offered a climate that was like the climate of Greece, but no food and scarcely any water, no dangers but a vast intangible resistance. They cut down the trees but there were always more trees, they burned them and they suckered. When a man wandered into the bush it closed over him like water and he was lost in its vast anonymity. The soil grew the imported seeds grudgingly;

10

they flourished for a little while then the sun withered them or they just died of despair. Hostility to man ran under the soil, it was in the clear air.

What the first settlers did not realize was that the resistance they met in the apparently open face of the country was perfection. They had broken into a world fully evolved, a system so close-knit, so completed that there was no place in it for them. Centuries had weeded out the weak in the flora and the fauna. In isolation they had worked out their destiny. The animals, the birds, the insects, the trees and the plants were exquisitely adjusted to their environment, a seamless creation, and there was no provision for man, the struggling and the incomplete, with his whole being fashioned by a different climate, attuned to a different earth. He needed all the force of his civilization to break his way through the mysterious resistance of a continent, and having conquered it, he has had to be conquered by it to make the new world of white Australia.

2.

PROCESSION

ON 26th January 1788, a brilliant cloudless summer day, a small party of officers and workers landed at Sydney Cove, and set to work clearing the ground, erecting a few tents and putting up a flagstaff. At sunset the Union Jack was hoisted and Phillip, Captain-General of the expedition, solemnly took possession of New South Wales from Cape York in the north to Van Diemen's Land in the south and as far west as the 135th degree of east longitude, in the name of the British Crown.

A thousand people set to work to tame a continent, to begin life again in the new world at scratch. Most of them had little aptitude and less heart for the adventure. The majority were prisoners. The detachment of marines who came to guard them were all volunteers, but they quickly repented their bargain. This was no Eldorado, no tropical paradise. It was two and a half years before help arrived from England. The spirit of one man, Phillip, held the little community together. Famine came, and recurred in diminishing force for a quarter of a century. It took twenty-five years to pierce the mountain barrier which separated the semi-barren littoral from the rich plains of the interior.

Australian history has a zodiac of its own. The first five years, prosaic and grim, were under the sign of the Cooking Pot, one of those common iron pots that appear so often in the despatches. In the riotous and colourful years that follow, it is under the sway of the Rum Bottle, whence it passes for a brief time under a marine emblem, the Whale, to enter one of its major periods in the late 'twenties, the 'thirties and 'forties, under the Sign of the Golden Fleece. Next in the 'fifties comes the Nugget, then a long constitutional period under the Mace, with a sudden rising of the Sword in 1914. After that followed a many-faced period of industrial expansion, the Smoke Stack, and now there has risen in our sky again, not the Sword but the monstrous constellation of the Tank and the Bomber. The periods interlace and grow out of one another, for the story is an organic whole, something that has been lived.

The famine and isolation of the early years resulted in a military autocracy. Rum provided the symbol of its monopoly, the currency of the colony, the soporific which bought the people's acquiescence. For a brief maritime interlude it looked as if the whaling industry in the unexploited South Seas might rescue the colony from the doldrums of rum. But greed and high duties quickly destroyed it. In 1810 Lachlan Macquarie came as governor to the colony. He broke the power of the military caste by raising up a class of small landowners dependent on government. He established a civil state and conceived a future, not glorious but stable, of a self-supporting agricultural community.

A new factor disrupted this dream and changed Australia's destiny. The fine wool industry had been born at Camden, a grant on the fringe of the settlement. Officially frowned upon, it prospered. The dry Australian pastures produced a wool as fine and strong as any that came from Spain or Saxony. The Industrial Revolution was raising England to a position of commercial strength as the premier manufacturing country of the world. There was a shortage of wool to feed her looms. Australia, the black sheep of the Empire, acquired a new significance. Her fleece was golden. In those days of primitive transport wool was the only commodity that she could export with profit. In the 'twenties, 'thirties, 'forties of last century the sheep was the sole, uncrowned king of the continent. Grazing displaced agriculture, the big landowner the peasant farmer. In the interests of the sheep, who must have wide pastures, the mountain barrier was surmounted. Men seeking water and grass for their flocks pioneered the hinterland. In the interests of the sheep inland Australia was explored and conquered. Sheep founded Melbourne. It was a pastoral age and it seemed as if it might continue in its tranquillity for ever.

But a dramatic event came to change the face of history once again. In 1851

12

gold was discovered first in New South Wales and then in the newly separated state of Victoria. A world whose imagination had already been warmed by the Californian gold rushes, responded to the new allure. In four years the population increased fourfold, in ten years £80,000,000 worth of gold was taken out of the ground. The type of the population was changed. A great impetus had been given to urban development and progress was accelerated in every field.

Until 1850 Australian life was only in outline, as it were. Self-government had made a tentative beginning in 1842. In 1850 the Australian Colonies Government Act was passed by the Imperial Parliament. It separated Victoria from New South Wales and empowered each of the five existing states to frame its own constitution. A few years saw the setting up of four independent legislatures.

Already in the 'sixties Australia was in the forefront of political and social experiment. New land laws were passed unlocking the country to small settlers, the principle of one man one vote was put into practice, the secret ballot, payment of members of parliament, industrial arbitration and wages board experiments followed. New Zealand outstripped South Australia by one year in the enfranchisement of women, the first country in the world to adopt the principle.

The years till the end of the century saw first a clarification of the separate states' needs and aims, a drawing apart, and then a drawing together, a general growing wish for federation. Not without long bargaining, the states, now numbering six, united at last and with the beginning of the new century the Australian Commonwealth came into existence. It was the splendid climax of a period of growth.

The first years of the century saw the development of the national theme. In 1908 the site of the Federal capital was chosen at Canberra and the first million spent on it. In 1911 the Australian Navy came into existence, a few years later the transcontinental railway linked east and west but before it was finished a new sign had arisen in the Australian zodiac. A world war had broken out and Australia came under the Sword.

In October 1914 the first convoy of Australian troops left for Egypt and on the 25th April 1915 Australian soldiers were taking their part in the landing at Gallipoli. Masefield wrote of them, "They were the finest body of young men ever brought together in modern times. For physical beauty and nobility of bearing they surpassed any men I have ever seen." Later, Australians were to fight with distinction in France and Palestine. Out of a population of five million Australia sent 320,000 men overseas and 60,000 did not return. In money alone she spent £350,000,000.

Out of the war came a great impetus to industry, a virtual end of isolation, Dominion status and now another war. . . .

3.

TABLEAU

AUSTRALIA TODAY

THE procession has only begun. At 153 Australia is still the young heir of all the ages. But heir is not quite the right word, it strikes a wrong note. Our progress is not to be measured in what we have received, or the skill with which we have imitated older civilizations, our cities piled against the sky, our machine-made sophistication, our imported decor. . . . Rather is it measured by our contribution and by our *rapprochement* to our environment. The earth that was so strange and hostile to the first settlers is gradually becoming ours. Its beauty, that is like no other beauty on earth, is becoming a part of our flesh, its strangeness is becoming not only familiar but a haunting magic. Australian eyes can see the beauty of the Australian scene, the infinite variety in its monotone, the fugitive grace of the eternal gum tree, pencilled on the living air. The first settlers were at utter variance with "the wretchedest country on earth." Gradually an understanding has grown up. That is progress. No people is ever a nation while it is out of touch with the earth upon which it lives. The story of that *rapprochement* is, very largely, the story of Australian culture and art. The community between the Australian soil and the Australian people is finding expression in a literature that is every year more and more unself-consciously Australia, and in the graphic arts. It is neither accidental nor insignificant that much of the finest and most famous work done by Australian painters has been in landscape. In music the movement has been more tardy, the interpretative side overwhelms the creative. In architecture, less again. As yet it is hardly an exaggeration to say that there is no essentially Australian architecture unless it be the bark hut which blends unself-consciously into the landscape. To build costs money and requires coöperation. The architect has not the free field that the artist has with his canvas. Most buildings have in

14

hard practice to be a compromise of tastes; the compromise runs naturally to the imitative or, where economy is strictly necessary, to the machine-made design. Similarly the motion picture needs money, a lot of money, and that makes it timid. There is a different life to be recorded here, new patterns of living, and a scene that photographs better than a society beauty, but they are not being recorded. The theatre seems almost dead; it too requires money and money is conservative.

We have been accused of cultural poverty. There is a pause which may be interpreted in terms of lethargy or it may be something more hopeful, a clearing of the stage, a freeing of mind and eye, so that our own indigenous culture, already strong in some phases, in germ in all, may have open road. There is another factor. When the total population of the Commonwealth is considered, the number of great names and of successful men and women in art, science and industry that Australia has given to the great world is very high. The rewards are greater overseas. Australia is the poorer for their going, not only in the definite loss of their services but in the weakening of public opinion at home. They pay the price of exile and the exile's mind.

Australia has paid her entry fee to the community of nations by the products of her soil, by her contributions to the theory and practice of social justice, by the work of her artists and craftsmen and, most important, by the preservation of a quiet mind.

SURVEY OF AUSTRALIAN ART

I. ABORIGINAL ART OF AUSTRALIA

BY MARGARET PRESTON

THE aborigines of Australia have always been regarded as in the lowest branch of civilization. That this is not the case, is shown by a study of their native art. Their rock paintings are true murals, and their geometric designs are spontaneous and symmetrical. Their work is either hyperrealistic, naturalistic or symbolical. They paint in three ways: freehand, stencilling or impressing. The last method is by putting the feet into wet pigment and impressing them on the surface to be decorated.

They have many ways of expressing themselves as artists; the bark painting in this exhibition is one of them. For this work, a piece of bark is stripped from a tree, heated and then pressed flat. The design is first grooved and lined round with colour, and then filled in with many intricate lines. The work is generally done in yellow and red ochre, helped with pipe clay. In all cases the dark brown of the bark serves as a background. Their brushes are of twigs chewed to make them pliable. In the examples shown, their hyperrealism is very evident. The outlines of the animals are strongly drawn and also the internal edible parts. They never show the internal anatomy of man, as they place him on a different plane from that of animals. The drawing of the figure with the arms outspread is symbolical; it stands as one of their spirits who walks by day and sleeps upside down in paper bark trees or bamboos. Their work never aims at perfection, but only a semblance of it.

Australia is the only country in the world in which rock painting still flourishes as the normal expression of its aborigines. This painting must not be judged from its technical quality, but from its introspective character. The drawings and rock carvings are a truthful art; they are realism in a wider sense than that recognized by European art.

Aboriginal art represents not only objects but essential truths which may or may not be visible to the human eye. The aboriginal artist arranges his colours in a definite order, and every tribe has its own characteristic mode of expression. The paintings of the natives of the Northern Territory, for

16

example, differ in subject and colour from those of the Kimberley district. The paintings of the natives of the Kimberley district differ in subject, colour and totemism from those of New South Wales. This holds good for the carvings and drawings. Their symbolism is infinite.

The study of the work of the Australian aborigines contains limitless possibilities for the artist. The symbolism expressed through its tribal totems opens up a new world.

II. THE FIRST BRITISH ARTISTS IN AUSTRALIA

(Acknowledgments are made to The Story of Australian Art *by William Moore, for much of this material.)*

ONE can scarcely expect that the best art of the period would be called upon to depict and record the discovery and settlement of a new continent. The nation's most accomplished artists did not accompany the early British navigators who visited Australia, so in our earliest art we have no works by great masters.

However slight or immature, the drawings and paintings of Australia by the first white men are valuable as records, and the small selection in this exhibition is typical of the period.

Most of the early navigators who sailed to Australia either drew or had artists with them. Although most of the work went back with them to England, many illustrated journals and originals have since found their way back to Australia and are now in the Mitchell Library and the William Dixson Gallery Collections in Sydney.

Amongst those who sailed with the first fleet in 1788 were John Hunter, "second" Captain on the *Sirius;* Philip Gidley King; John White, principal surgeon; Lieut. William Bradley, R.N., 1st Lieut. on the *Sirius;* George Raper, a midshipman on the *Supply,* and Surgeon Arthur Bowes and Lieut. Watts on the *Lady Penrhyn.* They were all capable as draughtsmen and most of them have left valuable records in journals or in sketches.

The first British artist to make a picture in Australia was Sydney Parkinson, who was the natural-history draughtsman on Captain Cook's *Endeavour.*

During its voyage he industriously made nearly one thousand drawings. He made the only study connected with the landing at Botany Bay, "Two Natives of New Holland advancing to Combat." He drew the "Careening of the Endeavour," the only contemporary picture of the vessel, drawn when she was careened after striking a rock off the Queensland coast.

During Cook's second voyage, William Hodges, topographical artist, and George Forster, natural-history draughtsman, accompanied him, and on his third and last voyage on the *Resolution* John Webber made drawings. Webber is known for his picture of the "Death of Captain Cook" made famous by the engraving by Bryne and Bartolozzi. The painting is in the William Dixson Gallery, Sydney.

Benjamin West, President of the Royal Academy, selected William Westall to accompany Captain Flinders as an artist, and he made numerous sketches in water colour and pencil.

The earliest painting of Sydney Cove is by Thomas Watling, a convict who arrived in Sydney in 1791. The picture was painted in 1794, the seventh year of the settlement. Its historical associations outweigh its art interest.

Writing in *Australian Landscape Painters of Today*, Mr. James S. Mac-Donald says: "When the early-comers to Australia first took in our landscape, they became aware of something wholly different from any other they had ever before seen.

"In the first place, the shores on which they landed grew trees of large size and of plenty of variety. This happens almost nowhere else in the world; yet all around Australia's 12,000 mile coast it is possible to stand a few yards back from where the sand begins and see, through the irregular frame made by ti-tree, eucalyptus, banksia and other fascinating tree things, the Pacific, Indian or Southern Oceans.

"Some of these trees persisted far into the interior and along the coast indefinitely and with little change of character—the most ubiquitous being the eucalyptus, our beloved 'gum tree,' exclusively ours! Wattles, as 'mimosas,' grow natively elsewhere, but the gum tree is all and solely Australian. Latitude and altitude cannot keep it out of any Australian landscape, and it has more shapes than any other tree growing in this earth. Indifferently it grows out of sand, rocks, loam, clay, gravel, swamps or the snow and in each case it takes to itself a different form; bark, trunk, limbs, leaves and their texture and density all varying.

"Where the first-comers anchored, the land about was of small elevation.

18

Further back were low, rounded rises covered with growth and purply-blue in tint. The local colour was of a browny-grey-green, in strange contrast to the succulent verdure left behind in other lands, whether at Home, or at places of call.

"Monotony must have been one of the first impressions on the pioneers that this green landscape made. Yet, in spite of this, it was so much a thing apart that, from the earliest times, persistent attempts were made to record its weird yet fascinating appearance."

The first real patron of the Arts was Governor Lachlan Macquarie who attached John William Lewis, an artist and naturalist, to various expeditions as "official artist." Lewis, who arrived in Sydney in 1800, offered to paint miniatures at 5 guineas and portraits at 40/-. He also started an art school. As he had little response, his wife helped by running "The Bunch of Grapes," an inn and store.

Macquarie also recognized the artistic ability of Francis Greenway by securing his pardon and making him Government Architect. Greenway had been transported for "hiding his effects during bankruptcy." He left a series of delightful churches, courthouses and other buildings which have never been equalled in Australia, and still remain as a standard of fine design and proportion. They resemble the early Colonial Georgian architecture in America.

In the early days, artists were found in all classes of the community—governors, a bishop, scientists, architects, surveyors, explorers and military and naval officers. In a brief survey one can only select typical examples, to build up the background of the early artists.

Amongst the artists who arrived in Sydney was John Eyre, a convict who did comprehensive views of Sydney, some of which were reproduced in London.

Joseph Lycett, transported to Sydney in 1810, was convicted on a charge of uttering forged notes. He practiced his particular art again in Sydney and was sent to the Newcastle mines. While so engaged he was allowed to paint the altar piece for the church being erected. He was also responsible for a three-light window in the Newcastle Cathedral. He was given a conditional pardon.

Richard Read, Sr., was the first portrait painter of any standing. He opened a drawing school in 1814. He painted Governor Macquarie. Richard Read, Jr., who arrived in 1819, advertising that he had no connection with anyone of the same name, painted many miniatures before daguerreotypes became known in Sydney.

The city of Hobart must have had a macabre fascination in those days, with beauty and grimness side by side. Both Hobart and Port Arthur had picturesque settings for penal settlements. William Barlow Gould, originally employed at Spode's Potteries, was transported thither in the 'twenties. There is a good example of his work in this exhibition.

Thomas Bock was an engraver and painter who did drawings after the style of Sir Thomas Lawrence in Hobart in 1824. He had the sinister duty of making pencil portraits of malefactors about to be hanged.

Quite unexpected people came to Australia in those days. For instance, one wonders what moved John Glover to go to Tasmania in 1831 with his children, at the age of sixty-three. Glover was the founder and once president of the old water-colour society, and one of the best-known artists of his time.

After Glover, there was Benjamin Duterreau, originally an engraver, who became a painter, and emigrated to Western Australia at the age of sixty-five. He settled eventually at Hobart in 1832. Nothing deterred these early colonists from a fresh adventure late in life!

Imagine the excitement in Hobart when it became known that the celebrated Thomas Griffiths Wainewright was there. Artist, regular exhibitor at the Royal Academy, writer, dandy, forger and poisoner, Wainewright was sent out in 1837. There are a number of his portraits in Hobart, one of which is included in this exhibition. Famous authors have written about him or used him; Charles Lamb, De Quincey, Lytton in *Lucretia*, Dickens in *Hunted Down*, and Oscar Wilde in his essay, *Pen, Pencil, and Poison*.

John Skinner Prout, who with Lieut. Simpkinson de Wesselow did some of the best drawings and water colours of Hobart, painted homes of pastoralists. Prout brought a lithoplant with him in 1843 and issued large litho-views on Tasmania, Melbourne and Geelong. Prout's drawings had more quality than Conrad Martens' and he was a first-rate artist of the period. De Wesselow originally served in the Navy. He is well represented in the Hobart Gallery by an excellent series of water colours and drawings.

The best known and the most prolific of the early artists is Conrad Martens, who came to Sydney in 1835. In his lifetime his paintings were sold for a few guineas, whereas today, an original by him is worth anything from 75 to 150 guineas. His drawings, sketches and water-colour drawings are superior to his overworked or completed works. There are many originals by him in the Mitchell Library and the Dixson Gallery, Sydney.

An outstanding personality, William Light, son of an English merchant captain and a Malay princess, was artist, musician, mechanist, seaman and soldier. He was intelligence officer on the staff of the Duke of Wellington in the Peninsula, and Surveyor-General of South Australia in 1836, when he selected the site of Adelaide. There is a first-rate self-portrait by him in the Adelaide Art Gallery.

Equally well known and equally prolific as Martens was Samuel Thomas Gill who arrived with his parents in Melbourne in 1839. He made numerous sketches in Adelaide, in Melbourne and on one of the goldfields, and was the most popular artist of the 'fifties.

Another artist of distinction in the early period was Oswald Brierely who was eventually appointed Marine Painter to Queen Victoria in 1874 and who received a knighthood. He visited Sydney in 1842 on a cruise on Benjamin Boyd's *Wanderer*. He managed Boyd's whaling enterprises at Twofold Bay. He was a typical marine artist of the day and his work is in the art gallery and the Mitchell Library Collection, Sydney.

Then there was William Dexter, who arrived in Sydney in 1852. He was an apprentice at the Derby China Factory, lived in Paris, worked in London and Nottingham. In Sydney he did anything from painting signs to restoring pictures and teaching drawing. He really was a most accomplished painter; his "Dead Birds," now in the National Art Gallery, Melbourne, was shown at the Royal Academy in 1851.

Finally, the goldfields attracted varied types to Australia in the 'fifties. One artist was Edward La Trobe Bateman, a friend of Rossetti and the Pre-Raphaelites, who made numerous drawings on the goldfields.

Another one, Eugene Von Guerard, whose father was Court painter to Emperor Francis I of Austria, was attracted to the Ballarat goldfields and made a large number of paintings and sketches.

A strange interesting motley of artists, when you review them, to be found in the new continent. The life from the foundation in 1788 up to the 'fifties offers much inspiration for artists—what material for murals, pictures, ballet, drama, as yet practically untouched.

III. FOUNDATION OF AN AUSTRALIAN SCHOOL

(Acknowledgments are made for much of the material in this section to the writings of J. S. MacDonald in Australian Landscape Painters of Today.*)*

A FRENCH SWISS named Louis Buvelot may be said to have been the inspiration of the Australian School of Painting. Coming to Australia in 1865 he made an honest effort to set down the unfamiliar landscape as he saw it. He showed much independence of observation and presentation, and his handling had some fine qualities of painting. He had little imagination; but he painted well according to the standards of the academies. This made him see the depictive worth of the new tree forms, the silveriness of the tones of the bush, the unusual high key that prevailed. His endeavours fired others, and in Victoria the Australian School was born.

What Buvelot started Roberts developed, having McCubbin as a strong helper. Urged by Roberts, the painters there tabooed studio-painted landscapes and worked in the bush, aiming at truth of tone and colour-values. For the first time in painting the bush was keyed to its right tone. These zealots worked in Melbourne until Roberts came to Sydney and discovered Conder at the same time as McCubbin, remaining in Melbourne, found Streeton. These four founded landscape painting as it is known in Australia today. Roberts may be regarded as its father.

Julian Ashton had then arrived in Melbourne, but he soon came to Sydney to settle. He had not the same human material to work on that Roberts had, but in the main his creed was the same, and his influence has been like in kind if less in degree.

Starting with high gifts Streeton soon produced work of a high order, and after fifty years he still predominates. He has shown us our land as no one else has done.

Streeton still remains the greatest influence in landscape painting in Australia. The first to reveal the "skin" of the country, no one yet has more successfully portrayed the great spaces, the closely timbered ranges, the fertile valleys, the strong sunlight, and above all the colour of Australia. To Streeton, blue and gold is the predominating Australian colour scheme. He paints with gusto, using a free brush, and he renders the shimmering blue distances with their exact aerial quality.

McCubbin was a painter who brought to landscape painting a touch of love that had difficulty in expressing itself fully, but the implication is there, warm, unselfish and gentle.

Two other painters, but slightly later, of that time, Walter Withers and David Davies, were of a like cast of spirit. Rural scenes, not too far afield, were their subjects.

As far as concerns Victoria, the next considerable influence was Max Meldrum. By reviving the drooping vitality of tonal values, and by forceful, unremitting injunction, he imbued his followers with the necessity of accepting his teachings. His regime admitted of no questioning, no doubts; and it was salutary. The painting of his followers is technically strong and living. Outstanding among them are A. E. Newbury, John and William Rowell and H. B. Harrison.

Heysen has painted another aspect of Australia. It was left for him to reveal the gum tree. He was concerned earlier with pastoral subjects, but later he became interested in painting and drawing the Flinders Range country, near Central Australia. He devoted much research to this work.

Gruner's work is less robust, but more sensitive. No one has portrayed the folds and contours of the landscape with greater skill.

Will Ashton, a robust painter, although he has painted Australia, is noted for his fine realistic series of France and Spain.

Sydney Long has retained the lyrical note and a pure colour sense in his work.

In oils, no fresh vision in landscape has been seen except in the work of John D. Moore, where modern methods and an individual outlook are noticeable, and also Roland Wakelin and Arnold Shore, whose work is referred to in the next section.

The outstanding artist, technically, in Australia is undoubtedly G. W. Lambert. Lambert, after twenty-five years' severe study in Europe, came back to Australia a stern critic of careless workmanship. He has had as strong an influence in New South Wales as Meldrum had in Victoria. Lambert was not restricted. He could draw and paint figure, landscape, still life, portraits, battle pieces, animals, murals and in addition he was a distinguished sculptor. He has painted a series of subject pictures of contemporary Australian life of which "Weighing the Fleece" in this exhibition is one.

Among figure men Longstaff remains one of the most distinguished portrait painters; Phillips Fox, Hugh Ramsay, W. B. McInnes, Rupert Bunny, Coates, and Quinn are also outstanding.

Australian water-colourists number Heysen, John D. Moore, B. E. Minns, Blamire Young, J. J. Hilder, Thea Proctor, Kenneth McQueen, Norman Lindsay, Lionel Lindsay, Harold Herbert, Daryl Lindsay, J. R. Eldershaw, Maud Sherwood. With the exception of McQueen, most of the water-colourists' work is on orthodox lines.

In still-life painting, Margaret Preston, Arnold Shore, Nora Heysen and Adrian Feint have worked with individuality and distinction. The Lindsay family are only given small representation in this exhibition. The subject matter being exclusively Australian debarred many artists from being shown. Norman Lindsay occupies an important place in the art development of Australia. "The Argument," one of his most remarkable pen drawings, needs no apology for its inclusion. This artist has also produced a notable series of etchings and dry points, water colours and oils. He is a romantic and a propagandist, and is not interested in local subject matter. His elder brother Lionel is also a distinguished wood engraver and etcher. His work is equally renowned in London and in Australia for his series of etchings on Spain. As the inclusion of prints created difficulty in such an exhibition as this, it is hoped that an exhibition of prints by Australian artists can be arranged at a later date.

Our landscape painting has yet a long way to go, even in the way of realism. Excepting in certain canvases of Streeton, the value key of Australia has not yet been won. Glistening, metallic leaves catching and letting through the light, blanched grass, white tree trunks, grey, green and grey-blue foliage, in one of the greatest expanses of clear dry atmosphere in the world, with the sun well overhead, all go to make it extraordinarily difficult and subtle. Decoratively, it is unique in opportunity among the world's landscapes, and it is wonderfully hard to depict—well.

IV. MODERN ART IN AUSTRALIA

BASIL BURDETT, writing in *Art in Australia* in 1938, which was devoted to "New Trends in Australian Art," says: The term modern art, nowhere very satisfactory or precise in its meaning, more than ever needs defining when it is used in Australia. Viewed from the angle of the *dernier cri* in Paris or London, there is little, if any, modern art in this country. . . . If we have in Australia little that might be correctly called modern art in the absolute sense, plenty of work is being done which differs widely from the generally accepted traditions here. Modern art dates in Melbourne from after the last war. Somewhere about 1925 Arnold Shore and William Frater began to be interested in post-impressionism through reproductions. . . . The result on Arnold Shore, who had been at the National Gallery School, was to release a natural colourist from the thraldom of tonal realism. Influenced chiefly by van Gogh his work underwent a drastic change. Frater was mainly influenced by Cézanne, like Wakelin in Sydney. He, too, turned his back on his artistic past at the call of the moderns. Frater evolved a sensitive, rather tenuous and personal style. Shore has had a wide influence, particularly when he joined George Bell in teaching.

George Bell, a recruit to modern ideas from academic ranks, is undoubtedly the leader of conscious modernism in Melbourne today and the major influence of the younger generation. An early associate of men like Lambert and Connard, dweller in Chelsea for many years and an accomplished realistic painter, George Bell's conversion to modernism was slower but even more complete than Shore's and Frater's. It was a conscious intellectual process, carefully reasoned by a keen artistic and general intelligence. He has been interested in every aspect of modern art.

He occasionally produces an abstract work. Abstraction he regards chiefly as formal exercise. Isabel Hunter Tweddle is a forceful, vigorous painter and a fine colourist. She was a recruit from the "Meldrum" School. Adrian Lawlor, a recruit from literature, is more intellectual in his outlook in spite of a strong emotional view, and more of an eclectic.

The outlook of Rupert Bunny, this fine and sensitive artist, who deserves that title far more than most Australian painters, is certainly modern compared with most of his Australian contemporaries. He is modern, as artists like Bonnard and Vuillard are modern in France.

Mary Cecil Allen came to modern art from the ranks of Meldrumism. She lives in New York, but during a brief visit to Melbourne she exercised a profound influence in favour of the new forms, both by teaching and lecturing, and did a great deal to make modern art more generally understood by both artists and laymen.

The younger generation in Melbourne shows more vitality and promise than at any time since that brilliant band of young painters, headed by Arthur Streeton and Tom Roberts, laid the foundations of Australian impressionism.

There is no ambiguity about painters like G. R. Drysdale, A. L. Tucker and Purves Smith. These three are unmistakably of their day.

Drysdale's dexterity is marked and he is an inveterate experimenter technically.

A. L. Tucker is almost self-taught, and his instincts have taken him at once to one or two modern painters with whom he is naturally in tune. An assiduous draughtsman, unceasing in his study of the figure, he has a fine sense of form; he is one of a group of Australian surrealists.

Purves Smith, another talented young painter, has a strong decorative strain. A vein of caricature shows in his work. He also has ventured into the dangerous realm of surrealism. Eric Thake is the prophet of the abstract among Melbourne's young moderns. Roger James has a closer affinity with English painters like the Spencers; Robert Pulleine, Nairne Butchart, Nutter Buzacott, Yvonne Atkinson all show a variety of influences new to Australia and there are painters like Madge Freeman and Elma Roach, who have brought back with them from Paris still another aspect of contemporary European painting, unfamiliar to Australian eyes.

Much of this, no doubt, sounds derivative and secondhand and may not indicate great originality. Much of it has a cosmopolitan and un-Australian flavour of European chic. Much of it is doubtless sterile and imitative. But at least it is experiment along what are new lines for Australian painters and an attempt to break the bonds of artistic conservatism.

Sculpture, too, shows the effects of modern ideas. Ola Cohn has demonstrated the virtues of a more simplified outlook on sculptural form, especially in her stone pieces; and sculptors like Reg Cordia, Edith Moore and Clive Stephen follow similar or even more drastic lines. It was bound to come. You cannot insulate a country from outside influences and legislate for its development along academic or traditional lines. If that had been done in the 'eighties we should not have had Streeton and Australian impressionism.

In Sydney, George Lambert discovered three artists who had been searching courageously for fresh methods of expression, Roland Wakelin, Grace Cossington Smith and Roi de Maistre.

Wakelin and De Maistre were the first artists to adopt and introduce modern art in Sydney. Their experiments covered a number of years. Wakelin paints interiors, still life, landscapes, portraits and figure subjects. He is a fine colourist and his work has great strength and individuality of outlook.

De Maistre was a travelling scholarship winner, who returned to Australia, but finding little understanding and encouragement at that time, returned finally to England, where he has made a name for himself. He has colour, design and taste.

Grace Cossington Smith and Helen Stewart are both distinctive artists. Enid Cambridge has a subtle colour sense in landscapes.

William Dobell is one of the most accomplished and interesting painters in Australia today. He won a Society of Arts Travelling Scholarship, studied in London and remained there until a few years ago, when he returned to Sydney. He exhibited the "Boy at the Basin" in the Royal Academy in 1933, a picture which drew the highest praise, at the time, from the critics.

Since then his work has developed. He was hard up in London; he lived, suffered with and was sympathetic with the poor. He made innumerable small studies, memory paintings, delightful examples, perfect little masterpieces, reflecting the life of the people, sometimes painted with a sardonic irony.

Since his return his work does not yet reflect an Australian reaction, but no doubt it will. He paints portraits and figure work, landscapes, street scenes—anything—and he can draw. He has great force. "The Tattooed Lady" in this exhibition is typical of his later work.

Eric Wilson, another scholarship winner lately returned, became converted to the modern method. He is particularly interested in "abstractions," as well as painting in the manner of the one exhibited, "Girl in Striped Dress."

Elaine Haxton, another native-born artist who came back to Australia, is an excellent designer, good draughtsman, as well as being an interesting painter.

One of the strongest influences in Sydney with the younger generation is Frank Medworth, an English artist of high standing, who two years ago became lecturer-in-charge of the East Sydney Technical College, which curious title translated means head art instructor of what is ostensibly the N.S.W. National Art School. Medworth is peculiarly suited for this position. Versed in all mediums, a practical and brilliant executant, he can paint in oil and water colour, engrave, etch and draw in pen, pencil or brush. His practical knowledge of industry and his interest in contemporary work make him peculiarly fitted for this position. Art in N.S.W. should progress and advance under his guidance.

There are many excellent designers in Sydney, chief of whom is Douglas Annand, who designed the displays in the Australian Pavilion for the New York World's Fair. Annand has never been away from Australia, which is surprising, as his work is completely sophisticated. He designs murals, book illustrations, cover designs, commercial work, posters, furniture, clocks—anything in fact.

Geoffrey and Dahl Collings, who returned recently from successes in London, and Alistair Morrison, who designed the cover and layout of this catalogue, and whose work in this direction was well known in London, and Gordon Andrews are other capable workers in this field.

Donald Friend is a brilliant young artist who spent two years in Nigeria, making studies, absorbing African art. He is an imaginative painter, whose work has a singular feeling of mystery and rich colour values. He is witty and ironical. He won a competition for an Australian ballet, the prize of which was awarded by Colonel de Basil when his company was in Sydney.

Other outstanding members of a vigorous younger group include Francis Lymburner and Francis Broadhurst.

Finally, it has been left for Margaret Preston to strike the one original note in the development of a new outlook for Australian art. Already having made a name for her decorative painting of wild flowers, she has studied the work of the aboriginal artists all over Australia. She has combined her research and knowledge of their outlook and design with her sophisticated study of European art, and applied it very successfully to the rendering of Australian landscape. In carrying out this idea she has set herself the limitation of using only those colours which are to be found in the particular district which she paints. In this way she enters fully into the outlook of the aboriginal artists, who were limited in their portrayal of colours by the clays and pigments which were found in the various areas.

The inclusion of her painting "Aboriginal Landscape" completes the cycle of this exhibition, which starts with the work of the aborigines, and ends with the influence of their work as a basis of a new outlook for a national art for Australia.

CATALOGUE OF EXHIBIT

(*In chronological arrangement*)

NOTE: *As the exhibition is too large to be conveniently circulated as a whole, a portion will be shown in Canada (denoted by an asterisk*) and not in the United States.*

PAINTINGS AND DRAWINGS

ABORIGINAL BARK DRAWINGS

From the East Alligator River District, Northern Territory.

1. *Three fish and a fruit bat.*
2. *Fish and turtle.*
3. *Three wallabies.*
4. *Bird.*
5. *Kangaroo hunt.*
6. *A spirit.*
7. *A spirit.*
8. *A spirit.*
9. *Three birds, and a man spearing one of them.*
10. *An echidna.*
11. *Hands, feet and a bird.*

National Museum, Melbourne.

ABORIGINAL PEN DRAWINGS

From Victoria. (White man's materials used.)

12. *Australians pursuing Chinese; an emu hunt.*
13. *Warriors dancing.*
*14. *Warriors.*

National Art Gallery, Victoria.

ANONYMOUS

15. *Sydney about the year 1815.* Oil.

Dixson Collection, Public Library of New South Wales.

JOHN EYRE (dates unknown)

It is only known of this artist that he was in New South Wales in 1804 and again in 1811, and that in 1812 he expressed his intention of leaving at the earliest opportunity.

16. *View of Sydney.* Oil.

Dixson Collection, Public Library of New South Wales.

SAMUEL THOMAS GILL (c. 1818–1880)

Born in Somersetshire, died in Melbourne. Belongs to the second period of Australian art, from 1840 to 1870, between the earliest topographers and the later more national school. Left a large body of work, both in landscape and genre, and is remembered chiefly as the artist of the Australian goldfields.

17. *General View of Sydney, 1861.*

18. *Subscription Ball, Ballarat, 1854.*

Dixson Collection, Public Library of New South Wales.

ROBERT RUSSELL (dates unknown)

Made the first survey of Melbourne, 1836–37; Clerk of Works in the Colonial Architects' Department till 1839; subsequently practiced privately as architect and surveyor.

19. *Melbourne from the Falls, 1837.* Water colour.

20. *Melbourne from the Falls, 1854.* Water colour.

Dixson Collection, Public Library of New South Wales.

J. ROPER (dates unknown)

No biographical data on this artist are available.

21. *Gold Diggers, Ararat, 1854.* Water colour.

Dixson Collection, Public Library of New South Wales.

PHILIP PARKER KING (1791–1856)

Born at Norfolk Island. Entered the Navy in 1808, becoming a Rear Admiral in 1855. In 1817 he was appointed to survey those parts of the Australian coast left unfinished by Flinders. Appointed to the sloop *Adventure* in 1825 for surveying the coast of South America. Lived in New South Wales from 1831.

22. *H.M.S. "Mermaid" watering party.* Water colour.

Public Library of Western Australia.

RICHARD MORRELL (dates unknown)

Son of parents who moved from England to Northam, Western Australia, in 1831.

23. *View of Freemantle, 1832.* Water colour.

Public Library of Western Australia.

JOHN GLOVER (1767–1849)

A prominent English artist of his time, being a founder, and subsequently president, of the Old Water Colour Society. Worked also in France under the patronage of Louis XVIII and the Duke of Orleans. In 1831, abandoning a prosperous though conventional career, he took up a large grant of land in Tasmania and moved thither with his family, living a patriarchal life and combining painting with agriculture.

24. *My Harvest Home.* Oil.

Tasmanian Museum and Art Gallery.

THOMAS GRIFFITHS WAINEWRIGHT (1794–1847)

Born in London, where he practiced both painting and journalism; a friend of Dr. Burney, Charles Lamb, Sir David Wilkie and Macready the actor. Wrote for Blackwood's Magazine and exhibited at the Royal Academy 1821–25. Finding his means insufficient to satisfy his tastes, he started on a career of forgery and subsequently murder by poison, three relatives being his victims. Eventually convicted of forgery, though never of murder, he was deported to Van Diemen's Land in 1837. During his convict days he was in demand as a portrait painter, working under the eye of an armed guard.

25. *Portrait of Mrs. Wilson.* Water colour.

Tasmanian Museum and Art Gallery.

Lieut. SIMPKINSON DE WESSELOW (dates unknown)

A nephew of the celebrated polar explorer, Sir John Franklin. Entered the Navy and was in charge of the Hobart Observatory in the 'forties.

26. *Kangaroo Bay, Hobart, 1846.* Water colour.

The Royal Society of Tasmania.

WILLIAM BARLOW GOULD (dates unknown)

Originally employed as an artist by Spode, the Staffordshire potter, he was transported for an unknown crime in the 1820's to Tasmania, spending some years in the Macquarie Harbour and Port Arthur penal settlements. After his release earned a living by painting still-life subjects in Hobart.

27. *Still Life, Fruit and Flowers.* Oil.

Lent by Charles Lloyd Jones, Esq.

? DOWLING (dates unknown)

Possibly this artist was Robert Dowling, son of the Rev. Henry Dowling of Launceston, trained at Leigh's Academy in London in the 1850's and subsequently an exhibitor at the Royal Academy. Returned to Tasmania and worked there and in Melbourne for many years, dying in London in 1886. The attribution to this artist is, however, doubtful.

28. *An Aboriginal Camp on Mingah Cattle Station.* Oil, painted 1870.

Warrnambool Art Gallery, Victoria.

CONRAD MARTENS (1801–1878)

Born in London of a German father and English mother, he was a pupil of A. V. Copley Fielding. Appointed in 1832 artist on H.M.S. *Beagle* during its survey of the South American coasts. Later settled in Sydney, where he worked and taught. Appointed librarian of the Parliamentary Library in 1863.

29. *Middle Harbour.* Water colour, painted 1876.

National Art Gallery of New South Wales.

LOUIS BUVELOT (1814–1888)

Born near Lausanne, Switzerland. Awarded medals at exhibitions in Berne, London, Philadelphia, and Melbourne. Known as the first artist who reproduced in paint the character of the Australian "bush."

30. *Vic orian Scene*. Water colour.

National Art Gallery, Victoria.

JULIAN ASHTON, C.B.E. (1851–)

Known as the "father of Australian art." Born in England of an American father and an Italian mother. Studied in London and at Julien's in Paris; exhibited at the Royal Academy. Moved to Melbourne 1878. Trustee of the National Art Gallery, Sydney, 1889–99; founder and president of the Society of Artists, whose medal he was awarded in 1924. Created C.B.E. 1930. Teacher of most of the outstanding contemporary artists of Australia.

31. *A Solitary Ramble*. Water colour, painted 1886.

National Art Gallery, New South Wales.

*32. *The Seas Immense*. Oil.

National Art Gallery, South Australia.

WALTER WITHERS (1854–1914)

Born in Staffordshire; trained at South Kensington and Julien's. Moved to Melbourne 1882, returning to Paris for further study 1887–88. A leading landscape painter; awarded the Wynne prize 1897 and 1900. President of the Victorian Artists' Society 1904–05; charter member of the Australian Art Association 1912; trustee of the National Gallery, Melbourne, 1912–14.

33. *Tranquil Winter*. Oil, painted 1895.

National Art Gallery, Victoria.

FREDERICK McCUBBIN (1855–1917)

Born in Melbourne; trained at the Artisans' School of Design and the National Gallery School, where he also served as drawing master, 1886–1917. Helped organize the artists' camp at Box Hill; exhibited in the first Impressionist Exhibition, Melbourne, 1889. Exhibited at the Paris Salon 1897. Several times president of the Victorian Artists' Society; charter member of the Australian Art Association, 1912. Influenced at first by Bastien LePage, he later fell under the spell of Turner.

*34. *Down on His Luck*. Oil, painted 1889.

National Gallery, Western Australia.

TOM ROBERTS (1856–1931)

Born in Doncaster, England; came to Melbourne in 1869. Trained at the National Gallery School there and at the Royal Academy School, London. After spending some years in Europe he returned to Australia in 1885, bringing with him a knowledge of impressionism which he imparted to McCubbin, Streeton and Conder, thus laying the foundation of an Australian school of painting. Founder and first president of the Society of Artists, 1895. Exhibited at the Royal Academy and the Paris Salon. His picture "Opening of the First Commonwealth Parliament" hangs in St. James' Palace.

35. *Shearing the Rams*. Oil, painted 1890.

National Art Gallery, Victoria.

36. *Bailed Up*. Oil, painted 1898.

National Art Gallery, New South Wales.

*37. *The Fossickers*. Oil.

National Art Gallery, South Australia.

WILLIAM LISTER LISTER (1859–   )

Born in Sydney; educated in England and France, 1868–88. Exhibited at the Royal Scottish Academy at the age of 17. President of the Royal Art Society, Sydney, since 1897; trustee of the National Gallery of New South Wales since 1900. Awarded the Wynne prize seven times, 1898–1925; awarded the Commonwealth Government prize, 1913, for a painting of the site of the Federal capitol.

*38. *Jamberoo*. Oil (one of the first settlements of New South Wales).

Lent by the artist.

Sir JOHN LONGSTAFF (1862–   )

Born at Clunes, Victoria. Studied at the National Gallery School and at Paris under F. Cormon. Won the first National Gallery travelling scholarship, 1887. Honourable mention at the Paris Salon, 1891, and at the Royal Academy, 1893. Official artist with the Australian forces in France in the first World War. President of the Australian Art Association from 1926; founder and first president of the Australian Academy of Art; trustee of the National Gallery, Melbourne, 1927; first Australian painter to receive the honour of knighthood, 1928. Awarded medal of the Advance Australia Association, 1933; Archibald prize 1925 and four times subsequently.

*39. *Morning Sunlight*. Oil.

National Art Gallery, Victoria.

BLAMIRE YOUNG (1862–1935)

Born in Yorkshire; educated at Cambridge. Went to Australia in 1885 as master of mathematics at Katoomba College, painting water colours in his spare time. Introduced decorative poster design into Australia 1895, but did not win wide recognition as an original artist till 1911, when he had a one-man show in Melbourne. Instructor in musketry and machine gunnery in England during the first World War. Exhibited at the Royal Academy; member of the Royal Society of British Artists and the Royal Institute of Painters in Water Colours. Art critic on the Melbourne *Herald*, 1929.

*40. *Rat's Castle*. Water colour.

National Art Gallery, New South Wales.

33

DAVID DAVIES (1863–1939)

Born at Ballarat, Victoria, of Welsh parents. Studied at the Ballarat School, the National Gallery School, Melbourne, and with Jean Paul Laurens in Paris, 1892–4. Has spent most of his life in Europe, his home being in Dieppe. Exhibited at the Salon, Royal Academy, New English Art Club, Carnegie Institute, Pittsburgh. Member, Royal Institute of Oil Painters.

    41. *Golden Summer*. Oil, painted 1888.

National Art Gallery, Victoria.

BENJAMIN EDWIN MINNS (1864–1937)

Born in New South Wales and studied under A. J. Daplyn, Julian Ashton and Lucien Henry. Well known for his black-and-white works. Drew for the *Illustrated Sydney News* and *Bulletin* and after 1895, in London, for *Punch, The Strand, Bystander* and other journals. Educated at the Royal Academy, New Salon and Royal Institute of Painters in Water Colours. A member of the Society of Artists, Sydney, and President of the Australian Water Colour Institute.

    *42. *The Pioneer's Camp*. Water colour, painted 1925.

National Art Gallery, Victoria.

Sir ARTHUR STREETON (1867–   )

Born at Mount Duneed, Victoria. Apprenticed in lithography; studied at the National Gallery School, Melbourne. Participated in the first Impressionists' Exhibition, with Roberts, Conder and McCubbin, 1889, and became a strong influence in the Australian school of landscape painting. Honourable mention, Salon of 1892; gold medal, 1909. Honourable mention, Carnegie Institute, Pittsburgh, 1913. Official artist in France during the first World War. Member, Royal Institute of Oil Painters. Awarded Wynne prize, Sydney, 1928. Knighted, 1937.

    *43. *Surveyor's Camp*. Water colour, painted 1896.

National Art Gallery, New South Wales.

    *44. *Sydney Harbour*. Oil.

National Art Gallery, Victoria.

    *45. *Passing Showers*. Oil, painted 1937.

National Art Gallery, New South Wales.

    45a. *Under the Peaks*. Oil.

National Art Gallery, New South Wales, through the
Australian Legation, Washington, D.C.

CHARLES CONDER (1868–1909)

Born in England, went to Australia at 15, working with a surveying party for two years. Worked on newspapers and attended classes at the Royal Art Society. Impressionist Exhibition, 1889. Died at Virginia Water, England.

46. *Departure of S.S. Orient*. Oil, painted 1888.

National Art Gallery, New South Wales.

PERCY LINDSAY (1870–)

Born at Creswick, Victoria. Studied under F. S. Sheldon, at the National Gallery School, Melbourne, and under Walter Withers. Most of his work has been done around Sydney. Also known as an illustrator.

*47. *The Bridge Builders*. Oil, painted 1927.

National Art Gallery, New South Wales.

GEORGE WASHINGTON LAMBERT, A.R.A (1873–1930)

Son of an American engineer and a Yorkshire mother. Born in St. Petersburg, his father being there helping to build the Trans-Siberian Railway. Came to New South Wales early in life; studied under Julian Ashton. Won the Society of Artists' travelling scholarship in 1900; studied in Paris and worked in London, partly as an illustrator. Exhibited frequently at the Royal Academy and New English Art Club.

48. *Across the Black Soil Plains*. Oil, painted 1899.

National Art Gallery, New South Wales.

49. *Sergeant of the Light Horse, Gallipoli*. Oil, painted 1920.

National Art Gallery, Victoria.

50. *Weighing the Fleece*. Oil, painted 1921.

Lent by Lieut. C. H. Rowan.

*51. *Portrait of an Australian Lady*. Pencil.

National Art Gallery, New South Wales.

52. *Australian Soldier*. Pencil.

Lent by J. R. McGregor, Esq.

Sir LIONEL LINDSAY, (1874–)

Born in Creswick, Victoria; pupil assistant at the Melbourne Observatory; studied at the National Gallery School, Melbourne. Cartoonist on the Sydney *Evening News*, 1903–26; subsequently spent much time in foreign travel. First president of the Australian Painter-Etchers' Society, 1921; trustee, National Gallery of New South Wales; charter member, Australian Academy of Art; knighted 1941. Known mainly for his etchings and woodcuts, he is represented in many galleries throughout the British Empire, Europe and the United States. Member, American Woodcut Society.

*53. *The Doctor's House*. Water colour.

National Art Gallery, New South Wales.

*54. *Chinon, France*. Drawing, 1930.

National Art Gallery, New South Wales.

MATTHEW JAMES MacNALLY (1874–)

Born at Benalla, Victoria. Studied at the National Gallery School in Melbourne and at

Herkomer's School, Bushey, Herts. Worked in Melbourne, Sydney and Adelaide, as artist, critic and lecturer. Member, Australian Water Colour Institute, Royal Institute of Painters in Water Colour (London).

*55. *Light*. Water colour, painted 1939.

National Art Gallery, South Australia.

NORMAN CARTER (1875–)

Born in Melbourne; studied at the National Gallery School. Apprenticed to a designer of stained glass, worked with a firm of decorators. Moved to Sydney 1903; lectured at Sydney University and East Sydney Technical College. Exhibited at the Royal Academy; medal, Paris Salon, 1913. Vice-president, Society of Artists; council member, Australian Academy of Art. In addition to portraits and landscapes he has done much work in stained glass design and murals.

*56. *Marauders*. Oil, painted 1940.

National Art Gallery, New South Wales.

MAX MELDRUM (1875–)

Born in Edinburgh; came to Melbourne at 14. Studied at the National Gallery School; awarded travelling scholarship, 1899. Studied in Paris, exhibiting at the Salon. After his return to Melbourne in 1913 he established the Meldrum Art School. Awarded the Archibald prize, 1939 and 1940. Member, Victorian Artists' Society; charter member, Australian Art Association, 1912; associate of the New Salon, Paris, 1927; trustee, National Gallery of Victoria, 1937. Lectured in the United States, 1931.

*57. *Interior*. Oil.

Lent by J. R. McGregor, Esq.

HOWARD ASHTON (1877–)

Son of Julian Ashton; born in London, came with his parents to Australia, 1878. Studied under his father. Formerly a member of the Society of Artists; subsequently member of Group 15, Sydney. Art critic, leader-writer of the Sydney *Sun*.

*58. *Golden Afternoon*. Oil, painted 1938.

National Art Gallery, New South Wales.

HANS HEYSEN (1877–)

Brought to Adelaide from Hamburg at the age of 6. Sent to Paris by private subscription, worked at Julien's and the Beaux Arts; exhibited at the Salon. Returned to Australia and devoted himself to interpretation of Australian scenery and subjects. Known as the foremost water-colourist of Australia, he has won great popular success, one of his exhibitions totalling £4,600 in sales. Awarded the Wynne prize (best landscape of the year shown in New South Wales) seven times; Crouch prize, 1931.

*59. *Brachina Gorge*. Oil, painted 1932.

Lent by Dr. R. S. Godsall.

*60. *Lifting the Harrow*. Water colour, painted 1922.

> Lent by J. R. McGregor, Esq.

*61. *The Farmyard Gum*. Water colour, painted 1936.

> National Art Gallery, New South Wales.

62. *Land of Oratunga, Flinders Range*. Water colour, painted 1932.

> National Art Gallery, South Australia.

HENRY GARLICK (1877–1910)

Born in Orange, N.S.W.; settled in Sydney at the age of 20, where he lived till his death. Studied with Julian Ashton and others. Won success as an animal painter.

*63. *Darby and Joan*. Oil, painted 1938.

> National Art Gallery, New South Wales.

AMBROSE PATTERSON (1877–   )

Born in Daylesford, Victoria; studied at the National Gallery School, also in Paris at Julien's and Colarossi's. For many years he has lived in Seattle, where he holds a position as teacher of painting at Washington University, Seattle.

64. *Collins Street, Melbourne, in 1911*. Oil.

> National Art Gallery, New South Wales.

SYDNEY LONG, A.R.E. (1878–   )

Born in Goulburn, N.S.W. Trained under Julian Ashton and taught with him at the Sydney Art School, 1907–10. Worked extensively in England and France, returning to Australia, 1925. Exhibited at the Royal Academy, Salon, Royal Scottish Academy, Royal Glasgow Institute. Awarded the Wynne prize, 1938. President, Society of Artists, Sydney, 1898–1901; president, Australian Painter-Etchers' Society; trustee, National Gallery of New South Wales since 1933.

*65. *Cloud Shadows, Narrabeen*. Oil.

> Lent by the artist.

FRED LEIST (1878–   )

Born in Sydney; studied under Julian Ashton. Illustration work for Sydney *Bulletin* and *Mail*, afterward for the *Graphic* in London, where he went in 1908. Exhibited frequently at the Royal Academy and Salon. Official artist in France during the first World War. Executed two murals for the Australian Pavilion at Wembley, 1924. Taught painting at the East Sydney Technical College. Charter member, Society of Artists, Sydney, and Australian Academy of Art.

*66. *Apotheosis of Australia*. Oil.

> Lent by Dr. R. M. Crookston.

H. SEPTIMUS POWER (1878–   )

Born in Dunedin, New Zealand; settled in Adelaide, 1898. Studied at Julien's under Laurens; official artist in France during the first World War. Frequent exhibitor at the Royal Academy. Member, Royal Institute of Oil Painters, Society of Animal Painters, London; charter member, Australian Academy of Art. Principally a painter of animal, hunting and war subjects. Represented in many public collections, among them the National Gallery, London.

*67. *Timber Hauling in Karri Forest*. Oil, painted 1939.

National Art Gallery, Western Australia.

CHARLES LLOYD JONES (1878–)

Born at Strathfield, Sydney; studied with Julian Ashton; subsequently in England. Returning to Australia, he went to work in the family firm of David Jones, Ltd., eventually becoming chairman of directors. Still finds time to paint, and exhibits regularly. Patron, Australian Academy of Art; trustee, National Art Gallery of New South Wales. First chairman of the Australian Broadcasting Commission.

68. *"Summerlees," Sutton Forest*. Oil, painted 1941.

Lent by the artist.

GEORGE BELL (1878–)

Born in Melbourne; studied there at the National Gallery School, also in London and Paris. Exhibited at the Salon, Munich, Royal Academy; official war artist in France. Awarded Crouch prize, 1928. President, Australian Art Association, Melbourne, 1924–6. Art critic, Melbourne *Sun Pictorial*. Became a convert to modern art, founding the Contemporary Art Group in Melbourne, 1932, and later the Contemporary Art Society; established a "modern" art school with Arnold Shore in Melbourne.

*69. *A Sea Beach*. Oil, painted 1930.

Lent by the artist.

J. MUIR AULD (1879–)

Born in Sydney; studied under Julian Ashton and J. S. Watkins, beginning as a black-and-white artist. Member, Society of Artists; charter member, Australian Academy of Art. Follower of the French Impressionists.

*70. *Spring, Thirlemere*. Oil, painted 1936.

Lent by the artist.

NORMAN LINDSAY (1879–)

Born in Creswick, Victoria. Started to draw for the Melbourne papers at 16; cartoonist on the staff of the *Bulletin* for many years. Worked in London and the United States, contributing to *Punch, Cosmopolitan* and many other publications. Original member, Australian Painter-Etchers' Society; member, Society of Artists, Australian Water Colour Institute. Perhaps the most versatile of Australian artists, having worked successfully in all painting and drawing mediums and also sculpture, etching, essays, novels and plays.

*71. *The Argument*. Pen and ink.

Lent by J. R. McGregor, Esq.

JESSE JEWHURST HILDER (1881–1916)

Born in Toowoomba, Queensland; educated in Brisbane. Worked as a clerk with the Bank of New South Wales. Later went to Sydney and studied with Julian Ashton, but as a water-colourist he was self-taught. Resigned from the bank in 1908 because of illness, and devoted himself to painting. After his death a memorial exhibition popularized his work, and it changes hands at greatly advanced prices.

*72. *Timber Getters*. Water colour, painted 1910.

National Art Gallery, New South Wales.

ELIOTH GRUNER (1882–1939)

Born in Gisborne, New Zealand, of Norwegian and Irish parents; brought to Sydney in infancy. Studied and taught under Julian Ashton. Became noted for his poetical versions of Australian scenery. Exhibited at the Royal Academy and Salon. Went to England and managed the Australian Art Exhibition at the Royal Academy, 1923. After some years in England his work became somewhat modernized. Charter member, Australian Academy of Art.

73. *Werribee Gorge, Victoria*. Oil.

Lent by Sydney Ure Smith, Esq., O.B.E.

*74. *Sea and Sunlight, Tamarana, N.S.W.* Oil, painted 1926.

Lent by R. R. Dangar, Esq.

*75. *Mt. Tennant, Canberra*. Oil.

Lent by W. G. Buckle, Esq.

76. *Weetangra, Canberra*. Oil, painted 1937.

(Awarded the Wynne prize, 1937; Society of Artists' award, 1937.)

National Art Gallery, New South Wales.

MARGARET PRESTON (Contemporary)

Born in Adelaide; studied at the National Gallery School, Melbourne; subsequently in Munich, Paris and London. Exhibited at the Royal Academy, New English Art Club, Beaux Arts and the International Exhibition, Carnegie Institute, Pittsburgh. During the war she learned pottery and taught it to shell-shock cases in Devonshire. This stimulated her to an interest in craft design which has influenced her later work. The first and best painter of Australian flora and aboriginal products.

77. *Aboriginal Still Life*. Oil, painted 1940.

National Art Gallery, Queensland.

78. *Australian Native Flowers*. Oil, painted 1939.

Lent by S. Ure Smith, Esq.

79. *Aboriginal Landscape*. Oil, painted 1941.

Yale University Art Gallery.

THEA PROCTOR (Contemporary)

Born in New South Wales; studied with Julian Ashton, also in London, where she worked many years. Returning to Sydney, she established art classes. Founded the Contemporary Group there and has championed the cause of modern art in Australia. Charter member, Australian Academy of Art.

*80. *Reclining Nude.* Water colour.

Lent by J. R. McGregor, Esq.

*81. *The Yellow Jug.* Water colour on silk, painted 1938.

National Art Gallery, New South Wales.

JAMES R. JACKSON (1886–)

Born in Palmerston, New Zealand; brought to Australia in childhood. Studied at the Royal Art Society's school, Sydney, later in Paris and under Brangwyn in London. Fellow of the Royal Art Society; taught in its school. Charter member, Australian Academy of Art. Portraits and landscapes.

82. *Hills of Sofala, N.S.W.* Oil.

Lent by the artist.

ROLAND WAKELIN (1887–)

Born in New Zealand; lives in Sydney. Studied with Roi de Maistre. Influenced by Cézanne, and is a leading exponent of the Modern movement in Australia. Member, Society of Artists, Contemporary Group, Sydney; charter member, Australian Academy of Art.

*83. *Romantic Landscape.* Oil, painted 1937.

Lent by the artist.

ISABEL TWEDDLE (Contemporary)

Born in Deniliquin, N.S.W.; studied in Melbourne under Frederick McCubbin and L. Bernard Hall. Influenced by the French Impressionists. Has held two exhibitions in London. President, Melbourne Women Painters.

*84. *The Otway Ranges.* Oil.

Lent by the artist.

*85. *Still Life.* Oil.

Lent by the artist.

JOHN D. MOORE (1898–)

Born in New South Wales; trained as an architect in Sydney, where he still practices. Worked in the office of Bertram G. Goodhue, New York, both before and after the war, during which he served with the Royal Engineers in France. Belongs to the progressive wing, both in painting and architecture. Member of the Contemporary Group, Sydney; vice president, Society of Artists.

*86. *Chaos, Sydney Suburbs*. Oil, painted 1928.

Lent by the artist.

87. *Sydney Harbour, 1936*. Oil.

National Art Gallery, New South Wales.

88. *Kurrajong Farm*. Water colour, painted 1936.

Lent by the artist.

MAUD SHERWOOD (Contemporary)

Born in Dunedin, New Zealand. Studied in Paris under Tudor Hart; has worked many years in Europe. Exhibited at the Royal Academy, both the Old and New Salons and in Italy. Member, Society of Artists, Australian Water Colour Institute; charter member, Australian Academy of Art.

*89. *Pomegranates—Still Life*. Water colour, painted 1939.

Lent by the artist.

VIDA LAHEY (Contemporary)

A native of Queensland. Studied at the National Gallery School, Melbourne, with Walter Withers and in Europe. Exhibited at the Salon, New English Art Club, International Exhibition, Paris, 1937. Member, Society of Artists, Australian Water-colour Institute, Contemporary Group, Royal Queensland Art Society; charter member, Australian Academy of Art.

*90. *Everlastings*. Water colour.

Lent by the artist.

DARYL LINDSAY, A.R.W.S. (1890–)

Born at Creswick, Victoria. At the age of 30 abandoned pastoral occupations and took up art seriously. Served with the A.I.F. in France. When making surgical drawings at the Sidcup Hospital he met Professor Henry Tonks, with whom he later studied at the Slade School. Exhibited at the Royal Academy. The first Australian elected associate of the Royal Water Colour Society, 1937. Curator of the Art Museum and Keeper of Prints, National Gallery, Melbourne, 1940.

91. *The Stone Crusher*. Water colour.

National Art Gallery, Victoria.

JOHN ROY ELDERSHAW (1892–)

Born in Sydney; studied under Ashton and Watkins; also in London. Exhibited, Royal Academy, Salon. Has lived and painted in Tasmania. Member, Society of Artists, Australian Water Colour Institute; charter member, Australian Academy of Art.

92. *Church on the Hill, Richmond, Tasmania*. Water colour.

National Art Gallery, South Australia.

HAROLD HERBERT (1892–   )

Born in Ballarat, Victoria; studied at the local technical school, where he later taught. Assistant art inspector to the Education Department of Victoria. Appointed official war artist in the Middle East for six months, 1941. Member, Society of Artists, Commonwealth Art Advisory Board; charter and council member, Australian Academy of Art.

*93. *The Plantation.* Water colour, painted 1927.

National Art Gallery, Victoria.

*94. *The Farm.* Water colour, painted 1930.

National Art Gallery, New South Wales.

MARY EDWARDS (Contemporary)

Born in Sydney; studied there and in Brisbane, London and Paris. Exhibited at the Salon at 19. Has painted largely in Oceania, the East Indies and India.

*95. *Daughter of Two Races.* Oil, painted 1938.

National Art Gallery, New South Wales.

ADRIAN FEINT (1894–   )

Born in Narrandera, N.S.W. Studied with Ashton after serving with the Australian army in France in the first World War. Most of his work was in black and white. He is widely known as a designer of bookplates, having won an American competition in that field. Several monographs of these have been published. Recently has devoted more effort to painting in oils. Member, Society of Artists; charter member, Australian Academy of Art.

96. *Morning in Onslow Avenue.* Oil, painted 1940.

National Art Gallery, Southern Australia.

*97. *Flowers in Sunlight.* Oil, painted 1940.

National Art Gallery, New South Wales.

97a. *Map of Sydney Harbour.* Oil.

Australian Legation, Washington, D.C.

LLOYD REES (1895–   )

Born in Yeronga, Queensland; trained at the Technical College, Brisbane, under Godfrey Rivers and Martyn Roberts; also at the Chelsea Polytechnic in London, and in Rome. Silver medal, Paris Exposition, 1937. Member, Society of Artists; charter member, Australian Academy of Art. Works extensively in black and white.

*98. *Autumn, Lane Cove River.* Oil, painted 1937.

National Art Gallery, Victoria.

GEORGE FINEY (1895–   )

Born in Auckland, New Zealand; trained at the Elam School in New Zealand and the Chelsea Polytechnic, London. Moved to Sydney, 1919; worked as cartoonist for the

Labour Daily, then for *Smith's Weekly;* is now chief cartoonist for the *Sydney Daily Telegraph*. Served four years in the first World War. Has held several one-man shows in Sydney and Melbourne.

    *99. *White Gum Blossoms*. Oil, painted 1939.

National Art Gallery, New South Wales.

KENNETH MacQUEEN (1897–)

Born in Ballarat, Victoria; trained at the Slade and Westminster Schools, London. Served with the army in the first World War. Exhibited at the Royal Academy and New English Art Club. Member, Society of Artists, Australian Academy of Art, Australian Water Colour Institute and Contemporary Group, Sydney; owns a farm in Queensland where he paints landscape in a fresh modern style.

    *100. *The Seed Drill's Track, Queensland*. Water colour.

National Art Gallery, Southern Australia.

    101. *Cabbage Gums and Cypress Pines*. Water colour.

Lent by the artist.

ARNOLD SHORE (1897–)

Born in Melbourne; spare time student and painter while working as stained glass craftsman and artist; studied at the National Gallery School and under Max Meldrum; teacher, lecturer, newspaper critic and professional painter. Crouch prize, 1938. Member, Australian Academy of Art, Society of Artists, Sydney, Twenty Melbourne Painters.

    *102. *The Vegetable Garden*. Oil, painted 1940.

National Art Gallery, Victoria.

    102a. *After Bush Fires*. Oil.

Australian Legation, Washington, D.C.

JOHN CHARLES GOODCHILD (1898–)

Born in London; moved to Adelaide, 1913. Studied at the South Australian School of Arts and Crafts and the London Central School of Arts and Crafts. Served in the first World War. Commissioned by the Commonwealth Government to make 36 drawings of Australian cemeteries in France; commissioned by Adelaide City Council to design historical panels in bas-relief for the city bridge. Member of the faculty of the South Australia School of Arts and Crafts since 1934. Member, Senefelder Club, Graphic Art Society (London), Australian Academy of Art.

    103. *Windsor, N.S.W.* Water colour.

National Art Gallery, New South Wales.

WILLIAM ROWELL (1898–)

Born in Melbourne; trained at the National Gallery School under McCubbin and Hall; also under Meldrum. Centenary art prize, Melbourne, 1934; Melrose prize

43

(South Australia) for portraiture, 1937; Crouch prize, 1939. Member, Twenty Melbourne Painters, Victorian Artists' Society, Australian Art Association, Australian Academy of Art.

    *104. *Grey Summer*. Oil.

National Art Gallery, Victoria.

HERBERT BADHAM (1899–   )

Born at Watson's Bay, Sydney; studied at the Sydney Art School under Ashton. Art instructor at East Sydney Technical College. A vigorous and realistic painter of contemporary life.

    *105. *Breakfast*. Oil, painted 1936.

National Art Gallery, New South Wales.

DOUGLAS DUNDAS (1900–   )

Born in New South Wales; started studying under Ashton at 22, while earning his living as a window dresser. Won the Society of Artists' travelling scholarship, 1927; studied at the Chelsea Polytechnic, London, also in France and Italy. Head teacher of drawing, East Sydney Technical College. Vice-president, Society of Artists; member, Australian Academy of Art.

    *106. *Sydney Harbour, from Rose Bay at Noon*. Oil.

Lent by the artist.

MAX RAGLESS (1901–   )

Born in South Australia. Largely self-taught, he has become an eminent painter of Australian landscape; also does etchings.

    *107. *Grampians Country, Victoria*. Oil, painted 1940.

Lent by the artist.

ARTHUR MURCH (1902–   )

Born in Sydney. Worked as an engineer, studying art at night and in his spare time. Won the travelling scholarship of the Society of Artists, 1925; studied in London and Italy. Returning to Sydney, he assisted Lambert on two important pieces of sculpture. Artist for a scientific expedition to Central Australia, 1933. Turning to sculpture, he recently won a competition arranged by Lord Lurgan for a memorial bas-relief to Dame Nellie Melba in the Sydney Town Hall.

    108. *Alpullargna*. Drawing, 1933.

    *109. *Kudingra*. Drawing, 1933.

National Art Gallery, New South Wales.

WILLIAM DOBELL (1899–   )

Born in Sydney; studied with Ashton; won the Society of Artists' travelling scholarship, 1929. Worked in London till 1939, exhibiting at the Royal Academy and elsewhere. Now art instructor, East Sydney Technical College; member, Society of Artists.

44

110. *Boy at the Basin.* Oil, painted 1933.

National Art Gallery, New South Wales.

111. *The Tattooed Woman.* Oil, painted 1940.

Lent by the artist.

GRACE COSSINGTON SMITH (Contemporary)

Born in Sydney; studied under A. Datillo Rubbo; also in England and on the Continent. Member, Contemporary Group, Sydney; charter member, Australian Academy of Art.

112. *Australian Wildflowers.* Oil, painted 1940.

National Art Gallery, New South Wales.

EILEEN CROW (Contemporary)

A native of Tasmania; studied at the Technical College, Hobart. Member, Tasmanian Group of Painters.

113. *Spring at Araluen, Tasmania.* Oil, painted 1938.

Tasmanian Museum and Art Gallery, Hobart.

JOSHUA SMITH (1905–   )

Born in Sydney; trained at the East Sydney Technical College and under Ashton at the Sydney Art School. Awarded a prize for the best drawing in any medium exhibited in connection with Australia's 150th anniversary, 1938. Member, Society of Artists.

114. *The Workman.* Oil, painted 1940.

Lent by the artist.

NUTTER BUZZACOT (1905–   )

Born in Perth, W.A. Studied under Ashton at the Sydney Art School and other Australian schools; also in London under Iain Macnab and Mark Gertler; also on the Continent. Crouch prize, 1940. Council member, Victorian Artists' Society.

115. *Warrandyte Landscape, Victoria.* Water colour, painted 1939.

Lent by the artist.

CONSTANCE PARKIN (Contemporary)

Born in Victoria. Won a travelling scholarship at the National Gallery School, Melbourne; studied at the Royal Academy School, London, and under André L'Hote, Paris.

*116. *The Village.* Oil, painted 1940.

Lent by the artist.

WILLIAM CONSTABLE (1906–   )

Born in Melbourne; studied at the National Gallery School and at St. Martin's Art School, London. Studied stage design extensively; member of "Whitehall Productions," Sydney, for which he designs sets. Also does easel paintings and illustrations.

117. *Design for an Aboriginal Ballet, No. 1.* Gouache.

118. *Design for an Aboriginal Ballet, No. 2.* Gouache.

Lent by the artist.

GEORGE RUSSELL DRYSDALE (1912–   )

Born in England, coming to Australia as a child. Had intention of farming after leaving Geelong Grammar School in 1927. First started to paint in 1935 and studied with George Bell in Melbourne, also at the Grosvenor School, London.

119. *The Paper.* Oil, painted 1940.

Lent by the artist.

119a. *Monday Morning.* Oil.

Australian Legation, Washington, D.C.

119b. *The Rabbiter and his Family.* Oil.

Australian Legation, Washington, D.C.

LINA BRYANS (Contemporary)

Studied with Frater in Melbourne, and is among the younger group of painters in that city, with a strong modern bias.

120. *Port Phillip Bay.* Oil, painted 1940.

Lent by the artist.

NORA HEYSEN (Contemporary)

Third daughter of Hans Heysen; born near Adelaide, S.A. Studied at an art school there and under her father; also 4 years with Bernard Meninsky, Westminster Art School, London. Now a resident of Sydney. Archibald portrait prize, 1938; member, Society of Artists.

*121. *Still Life, Apples.* Oil, painted 1937.

Lent by J. R. McGregor, Esq.

G. R. MAINWARING (1912–   )

Born in Adelaide; trained at the South Australian School of Arts and Crafts, of whose teaching staff he is now a member.

122. *Brown Hill Creek.* Oil, painted 1939.

National Art Gallery, South Australia.

ELAINE HAXTON (Contemporary)

Originally trained in sculpture at East Sydney Technical College; worked for two years as a fashion artist. Went to London where she worked as an illustrator and advertising lay-out artist. Visited the United States and Mexico, 1939. Member, Contemporary Art Society.

123. *Early Colonial Architecture.* Gouache, painted 1940.

Lent by the artist.

ERIC WILSON (1911–)

Born in Sydney; studied with Ashton; awarded the New South Wales travelling art scholarship, 1937. Studied in London at the Royal Academy and Westminster schools. Appointed to the faculty of the East Sydney Technical College, 1940. Member, Society of Artists.

124. *Girl in Striped Dress.* Oil, painted 1939.

Lent by the artist.

PETER PURVES SMITH (1913–)

Born in Melbourne; educated at Geelong Grammar School and Jervis Bay Naval College. Trained in art at the Grosvenor School, London, in Paris and in Melbourne under George Bell. Now a lieutenant in the B.E.F. in England.

125. *The Diplomats.* Oil, painted 1939.

Lent by the artist.

125a. *Kangaroo Hunt.* Oil, painted 1939.

Australian Legation, Washington, D.C.

NOEL WOOD (Contemporary)

As a revolt against a conventional art career, Wood left Adelaide and bought Bedarra Island off the north coast of Queensland, where he lives and paints its scenery and that of the neighbouring Dunk Island. Has had one-man shows in Sydney and Melbourne.

126. *Path to Banfield House, Dunk Island.* Oil, painted 1939.

National Art Gallery, Queensland.

FRANCIS BROADHURST (1914–)

Born in Melbourne; employed as a lithographic artist at 13, taking evening art classes in the Melbourne Technical School. At 23 started theatrical and social caricatures for a local paper. Moved to Sydney and won fame as an illustrator, having been commissioned to illustrate limited editions of the *Decameron*, Rabelais and Casanova.

127. *King's Cross, Sydney.* Pen and ink.

Lent by the artist.

LOUDON SAINTHILL (1918–)

Born in Hobart, Tasmania. Studied art at Melbourne Technical School, 1936–8; had his first show of ballet paintings in Melbourne, 1939. Travelled two and a half years with the Russian Ballet, designing decors and costumes. Exhibited at the Redfern Gallery, London, 1939, all his pictures finding buyers.

*128. *The Echoes;* design for a ballet. Gouache, painted 1940.

National Art Gallery, South Australia.

128a. *Design for a Ballet.*

Australian Legation, Washington, D.C.

RUPERT CHARLES WOLSTEN BUNNY (Contemporary)

Born in Melbourne; studied at the National Gallery School there and later in Paris under Jean Paul Laurens. Exhibited at the Old, New and Autumn Salons, the Royal Academy and at the Carnegie Institute, Pittsburgh. Member of the International Society of Sculptors and Painters (Paris).

128b. *Black Swans.* Oil.

Australian Legation, Washington, D.C.

ERIC THAKE (1904–   )

Born in Melbourne; studied with George Bell; paints only in spare time with small output. Works as commercial artist.

128c. *Happy Landings.* Oil.

Australian Legation, Washington, D.C.

MARY CECIL ALLEN (Contemporary)

Studied at the Melbourne National Gallery and at Gloucester, Massachusetts. Author of *The Mirror of the Passing World*, 1928, and *Painters of the Modern Mind*, 1929. Came to New York in 1927 and still living there.

128d. *Ring-barked Gum Trees.* Water colour.

Australian Legation, Washington, D.C.

SCULPTURE

Sir BERTRAM MacKENNAL, K.C.V.O., R.A. (1863–1931)

Born in Melbourne. Studied at the National Gallery School and with his father, an architectural sculptor; also at the Royal Academy School and in Paris. Worked as head of the art department in one of the pottery firms at Coalport, Shropshire. Returned to Melbourne, 1887; designed reliefs for the façade of the Victorian Houses of Parliament. Awarded honourable mention, Paris Salon, 1893, for his figure *Circe*. A.R.A. 1909, R.A. 1922, M.V.O. 1912, K.C.V.O. 1921. Designed the coronation medal and coinage of George V. Australia's most distinguished sculptor.

*129. *Reclining Model.* Bronze.

Lent by Sir Marcus Clark, K.B.E.

C. WEB GILBERT (1869–1925)

Born at Talbot, Victoria. First practiced sculpture on wedding cakes for a confectioner in Melbourne. Studied at the National Gallery School; went to London, 1914. Exhibited at the Royal Academy; his head *The Critic* purchased by the Tate Gallery, 1917. Executed memorial to the 2d Australian Division, St. Quentin, France; Flinders statue at Melbourne; colossal figure of a digger at Broken Hill.

*130. *The Digger.* Bronze, 1922.

Lent by Sir Marcus Clark, K.B.E.

DAPHNE MAYO (Contemporary)

Born in Queensland; studied under Godfrey Rivers and Ashton; Royal Academy School of Sculpture. First woman to be awarded the Prix de Rome. Commissions, Brisbane Town Hall, Public Library, Sydney. Member, Society of Artists, Australian Academy of Art. Awarded the Society of Artists' medal, 1938, in recognition of her services to art.

*131. *The Young Australian*. Bronze, 1930.

National Art Gallery, New South Wales.

RAYNER HOFF (1894–1937)

Born on the Isle of Man, son of an expert wood carver and mason. Studied at the Nottingham Art School, 1910–15. Served in France in the first World War, partly on topographical survey, making maps from aerial photographs. Entered the Royal College of Art, 1919, winning Prix de Rome, 1921. After 3 years in Rome he was appointed instructor in sculpture at East Sydney Technical College; eventually became head of the school and completely reorganized it. Commissions, Anzac Memorial, Sydney; South Australian war memorial.

*132. *Atalanta*. Bronze.

*133. *Mask*. Bronze.

National Art Gallery, New South Wales.

LYNDON DADSWELL (1908–)

Born in New South Wales; studied under Ashton and Rayner Hoff, Paul Montford at Melbourne, Royal Academy School. Wynne prize, 1934. Head teacher of sculpture, Technical College, Sydney, 1934. At present serving with the Australian forces in the Middle East.

134. *Aboriginal Head*. Bronze, 1939.

Lent by the artist.

BIBLIOGRAPHY

ABORIGINAL ART

BOOKS AND REPRINTS

BASEDOW, HERBERT. "Aboriginal rock carvings of great antiquity in South Australia" (with bibl. notes and plates). Reprinted from the *Journal of the Royal Anthropological Institute*, Vol. 44 (January–June, 1914). Imp. 8vo, pp. 195–210, pl. 17. London.

"Notes on the natives of Bathurst Island, North Australia" (with bibl. notes and plates). Reprinted from the *Journal of the Royal Anthropological Institute*, Vol. 43 (January–June, 1913). Ill., imp. 8vo, pp. 291–323, pls. 7–20. London.

CAMPBELL, WILLIAM DUGALD. "Aboriginal carvings of Port Jackson and Broken Bay," *Memoirs, New South Wales Geological Survey* (Ethn. ser. 1). Ill., map, roy. 4to, pp. v, 73. Sydney, W. A. Gullick, Gov't Printer, 1899.

DAVIDSON, DANIEL SUTHERLAND. "Aboriginal Australian and Tasmanian rock carvings and paintings" (with bibl.), *American Philosophical Society, Mem.*, Vol. 5 (1936). Ill., map, roy. 8vo, pp. xi, 151. Philadelphia.

"Preliminary consideration of aboriginal Australian decorative art" (with bibl.), *American Philosophical Society, Mem.*, Vol. 9 (1937). Ill., maps, roy. 8vo, pp. xiii, 147. Philadelphia.

ETHERIDGE, ROBERT, the younger. "The Dindroglyphs or carved trees of New South Wales" (with bibl. notes), *Memoirs, New South Wales Geological Survey* (Ethn. ser. 3). Ill., map, 4to, 104 pp., pl. xxxix. Sydney, W. A. Gullick, Gov't Printer, 1918.

GENNEP, ARNOLD VAN. "Dessins sur peaux d'opossum australiennes" (with bibl.), *Mus. Nat. d'Ethnog. des Pays Bas à Leyde*, No. 14. Ill., roy. 8vo, 9 pp., pl. 14. S'Gravenhage, 1907.

GODDARD, ROY HAMILTON. "Certain observations of aboriginal rock-carvings in the Wollombi district . . . [with] Interpretation of the drawings at Burragurra and Yango, by F. Slater" (with bibl. notes and plates). 8vo, pp. (1), 15, pl. 3. Sydney, S.C.A.M. Print, Sutherland, 1937.

Abstracts of papers read before the Australian and New Zealand Association for the Advancement of Science. Auckland meeting, Sec. F. January 14, 1937.

McCARTHY, FREDERICK DAVID. "Australian aboriginal decorative art" (with bibl.). Ill., 4to, 48 pp. Sydney, Australian Museum, 1938.

MATHEW, REV. JOHN. "Cave paintings of Australia, their authorship and significance" (with bibl. notes). Reprinted from the *Journal of the Royal Anthropological Institute*, 1893. 8vo, pp. 42–52, pl. 4. London, Harrison & Sons, 1893.

MATHEWS, ROBERT HAMILTON. "Aboriginal ground and tree drawings," *Science of Man. N.S.*, Vol. 1 (1898), pp. 185–187.

"Aboriginal rock paintings and carvings in New South Wales." Reprinted from the *Roy. Soc. Vic., Proc.* (1894), pp. 143–156. 8vo, pl. (2). Melbourne, Ford & Son, Printers, 1894.

"Aboriginal rock pictures in Queensland." Reprinted from the *American*

Philosophical Society, Proc. (1901), pp. 57–58. 8vo. Philadelphia? 1901?

"Aboriginal rock pictures of Australia." Reprinted from the *Roy. Geog. Soc. Aust'sia, Q'land Br., Proc.* 10 (1894–95). 8vo, pp. (1), 46–70, pl. (2).

"Australian ground and tree drawings" (with bibl. notes). Reprinted from the *American Anthropologist*, February, 1896. Ill., 8vo, pp. 33–49.

"Australian rock carvings" (with bibl. notes). Reprinted from the *American Philosophical Society, Proc.* (1897), pp. 195–208. 8vo, 14 pp., pl. (1).

"Australian rock pictures" (with bibl. notes). Reprinted from the *American Anthropologist*, July, 1895. Ill., 8vo, pp. 268–278, pl. (2).

"Pictorial art among the Australian aborigines" (with bibl. notes). Paper read before the Victoria Institute of London, December, 1899. 8vo, 20 pp., pl. 2. London, Harrison & Sons, Printers.

"Rock carvings and paintings of the Australian aborigines" (with bibl. notes). Reprinted from the *American Philosophical Society, Proc.* (1897). 8vo, pp. 466–478, pl. (1).

"Rock carvings of the Australian aborigines" (with bibl. notes). Reprinted from the *Roy. Geog. Soc. Aust'sia, Q'land Br., Proc.* 14 (1898–99). 8vo, pp. 9–11, pl. 1.

"Rock paintings and carvings of the Australian aborigines" (with bibl. notes), Pts. 1–2. Reprinted from the *Journal of the Royal Anthropological Institute*, November, 1895, May, 1898. 8 vo, pp. 145–163, 532–541, pl. (5). London, Harrison & Sons, Printers, 1895, 1898.

"Rock paintings by the aborigines in caves on Bulgar Creek, near Singleton." Reprinted from the *Journal of the Royal Society of New South Wales*, 1893. 8vo, pp. 353–358, pl. (3).

"Some rock engravings of the aborigines of New South Wales" (with bibl. notes). Reprinted from the *Journal of the Royal Society of New South Wales*, 1910. Ill., 8vo, pp. 401–405.

"Some rock pictures and ceremonial stones of the Australian aborigines" (with bibl. notes). Paper read before the Aust'sn. Association for the Advancement of Science. Ill., 8vo, pp. 493–498. Brisbane, A. J. Cumming, Gov't Printer, 1910.

MATHEWS, ROBERT HAMILTON and ENRIGHT, WALTER JOHN. "Rock paintings and carvings of the aborigines of New South Wales" (with bibl. notes). Paper read before the Aust'sn. Association for the Advancement of Science. 8vo, 14 pp., pl. (2). Brisbane, 1895.

WORSNOP, THOMAS. "Prehistoric arts, manufactures, works, weapons, etc., of the aborigines of Australia." Ill., 8vo, pp. xv, 172. Adelaide, C. E. Bristow, Gov't Printer, 1897.

"Pre-historic arts of the aborigines of Australia." Reprinted from the *Roy. Geog. Soc. Aust'sia, S. Aust. Br., Proc.* 2 (1886–88), pp. 9–32. Map, 8vo, 26 pp., pl. (11). Adelaide, E. Spiller, Gov't Printer, 1887.

PERIODICALS AND SPECIAL ARTICLES

BARRETT, C. "Cave hunting and what we found," *Aust. Mus. Mag.* (October–December, 1929), pp. 414–419. Ill.

BASEDOW, H. "Aboriginal art," in his *Australian Aboriginal* (1925), pp. 297–358. Ill.

CAMBAGE, R. H. and SELKIRK, H. "Early drawings of an aboriginal ceremonial ground," *Journal of the Royal Society of New South Wales* (1920), pp. 74–78. Ill.

DALEY, C. "Artistic sense as displayed in the aborigines of Australia," pp. 427–436. *Australian and New Zealand Association for the Advancement of Science, Report.* Sydney meeting, 1911.

ELKIN, A. P. "Rock paintings of North West Australia," *Oceania* (October–December, 1930), pp. 257–279. Ill.

ETHERIDGE, R. "Remarkable rock shelter in the Milton District, N.S.W.," *Aust. Mus. Syd., Rec.* (January, 1904), pp. 80–85.

FRAZER, Sir J. G. "Rock paintings in West Australia" (with bibl. notes), in his *Totemica*, pp. 123–151. 1937.

GREY, Sir G. "Painted caves of the Australian aborigines," in his *Journals of two expeditions of discovery in North-west and Western Australia*, Vol. 1, pp. 201–206, 213–216, 259–264. Ill. 1841.

HALE, H. M. and TINDALE, N. B. "Further notes on aboriginal rock carvings in South Australia," *S. Aust. Nat.*, Vol. 10, No. 2 (February, 1929), pp. 30–34. Ill.

JACK, R. L. "On aboriginal cave-drawings on the Palmer goldfield," *Roy. Soc. Q'land, Proc.* 11 (1895–96), pp. 91–98. Ill.

LOVE, J. A. B. "Rock paintings of the Worrora and their mythological interpreta-tion," *Journal of the Roy. Soc. W. A.,* Vol. 16 (1929–30), pp. 1–24. Ill.

MOUNTFORD, C. P. "Aboriginal rock carvings in South Australia" (with bibl.), *Australian and New Zealand Association for the Advancement of Science, Report,* Vol. 19 (1928), pp. 337–366.

"Rock paintings at Windula, Western Australia," *Oceania* (June, 1937), 429–435. Ill.

SPENCER, Sir W. B. "Decorative art of the Melville Islanders," in his *Wanderings in Wild Australia*, Vol. 2, pp. 695–713. Ill. 1928.

SPENCER, Sir W. B. and GILLEN, F. J. "Clothing, weapons, implements, decorative art," in their *Native Tribes of Central Australia* (1938), pp. 567–635. Ill.

"Decorative art," in their *Arunta*, Vol. 2, pp. 551–578. Ill. 1927.

"Decorative art," in their *Northern Tribes of Central Australia*, pp. 696–743. 1904.

SMYTH, R. B. "Ornamentation," in his *Aborigines of Victoria*, Vol. 1, pp. 223–298. Ill. 1878.

TRYON, H. "Undescribed class of rock drawings of aborigines in Queensland," *Roy. Soc. Q'land, Proc.* 1 (1884–85), pp. 45–52. Ill.

New South Wales Geological Survey Records 1–3 (1889–1893). Various articles.

THE EUROPEAN TRADITION

PERIODICAL

Art in Australia. A quarterly journal devoted to the Fine Arts. Originally published by Art in Australia, Ltd. Founded in 1916 by Sydney Ure Smith who was its editor until 1938. Now edited by Peter Bellew; published by John Fairfax & Sons, Ltd.

BOOKS

The Julian Ashton Book. Sydney Ure Smith and Bertram Stevens, eds. Pub. by Art in Australia, Ltd., 1920. 600 copies, 9¾ x 7¼ ins., 28 plates in colour and black and white. Literary contributors, Hardy Wilson, Norman and Lionel Lindsay, Christopher Brennan. Pub. price, 12/6. Out of print.

Ashton, *Will, the Art of*. Art in Australia, 3d Series, No. 28 (June, 1929). 13 plates in colour, 22 plates in black and white. Articles by Hans Heysen. Pub. price, 12/6.

Australian Art Annual 1939. Sydney Ure Smith, ed. Pub. by Ure Smith Pty., Ltd. 11 plates in colour, 71 plates in black and white. Contains articles on the art of the year. A reference book concerning art galleries, art societies, art schools, etc. Pub. price, £1.1.0.

The Exhibition of Australian Art in London, 1923. Pub. by Art in Australia, Ltd. A record of this notable exhibition, with practically every picture reproduced. 200 illustrations in colour and black and white. 1,000 copies. Pub. price, £3.3.0. Out of print.

Australian Landscape Painters of Today. Sydney Ure Smith and Leon Gellert, eds. Pub. by Art in Australia, Ltd., Sydney, 1929. 20 plates in colour, 32 plates in black and white. Articles by J. S. MacDonald and Basil Burdett. Pub. price, £2.2.0.

Australian and New Zealand Etchings. Pub. 1923. A de luxe edition of Art in Australia, No. 9, including the first etching done in Australia by Conrad Martens. 12 copies. Pub. price, £5.5.0. Out of print.

A Contemporary Group of Artists. Art in Australia, 3d Series, No. 29 (September, 1929). 10 plates in colour, 23 in black and white. Articles by Basil Burdett and Ethel Anderson. Pub. price, 12/6.

Boyd (*Penleigh*), *The Landscapes of*. With Biography by James MacDonald; Foreword by Hugh Grant Adam. 11 plates in colour. 500 copies. 4to, wrapper. Melbourne, n.d. Price, 21/–.

Feint (*Adrian*) *Bookplates*. Introduction by the Hon. J. Lane Mullins, M.L.C. 110 copies. 21 plates, art boards. Palmtree Press, Sydney, 1928. Price, 30/–.

Fifty Years of Australian Art (1879–1929). By Members of the Royal Art Society, with a Commentary by George Galway. 20 illus. in colour, 100 in black and white. 4to, wrapper. Sydney, 1929. Pub. price, 7/6.

Finey (*George*), *Caricatures by*. Art in Australia, 3d Series, No. 38 (June, 1931). 46 plates. Articles by J. S. MacDonald and Lionel Lindsay. Pub. price, 3/6.

First Contemporary All Australian Art Exhibition, Roerich Museum, New York, 1931.

Gruner (*Elioth*), *The Recent Work of*. Art in Australia, 3d Series, No. 27 (March, 1929). 14 plates in colour, 24 plates in black and white. Article by Basil Burdett. Pub. price, 12/6.

Gruner's (*Elioth*) *Oil Paintings*. Art in Australia, 3d Series, No. 50 (June, 1933). 8 plates in colour, 8 plates in black and white. Articles by John Cam Duncan and J. S. MacDonald. Pub. price, 3/6.

Gruner (*Elioth*), *The Art of*. Sydney Ure Smith and Leon Gellert, eds. Pub. by Art in Australia, Ltd., 1922. 9¼ x 11¼. 600 copies, signed and numbered. 25 plates in colour, 17 plates in black and white. Articles on Gruner by Norman Lindsay and Julian Ashton. Pub. price, £3.3.0. Out of print.

Goodchild (*John C.*). *Drawings of Adelaide.* With 12 illus. 8vo, wrapper. Adelaide, 1924. Pub. price, 2/6.

Herbert (*Harold*). *Watercolours.* Art in Australia, 3d Series, No. 25 (September, 1928). 13 plates in colour, 24 plates in black and white. Article by J. S. MacDonald. Pub. price, 12/6.

Heysen (*Hans*), *The Art of.* Sydney Ure Smith and Bertram Stevens, eds. Pub. by Angus & Robertson, Ltd., 1920. Uniform with Streeton book. 31 plates in colour, 24 in black and white. Article on Hans Heysen by Lionel Lindsay. 1,500 copies. Pub. price, £2.2.0. Out of print.

Heysen (*Hans*), *Recent Watercolours by.* Art in Australia, 3d Series, No. 24 (June, 1928). 14 plates in colour, 25 plates in black and white. Article by Lionel Lindsay. Pub. price, 12/6.

Heysen (*Hans*), *Watercolours and Drawings by.* Art in Australia, 3d Series, No. 44 (June, 1932). 3 plates in colour, 17 plates in black and white. Articles by J. S. MacDonald and Hans Heysen. Pub. price, 3/9.

Hilder (*J. J.*), *The Art of.* Sydney Ure Smith and Bertram Stevens, eds. Pub. by Angus & Robertson, Ltd., Sydney, 1918. 29 plates in colour, 15 pen and pencil drawings, 5 photographs, 4to, board. Pub. price, £2.2.0.

Hoff's (*Rayner*) *Sculpture.* Art in Australia, 3d Series, No. 46 (October, 1932). 31 plates. Articles by Lionel Lindsay and W. B. Dalley. Pub. price, 3/9.

Johnson (*Robert*), *Landscapes by.* Art in Australia, 3d Series, No. 54 (February, 1934). 6 plates in colour, 16 plates in black and white. Article by B. J. Waterhouse. Pub. price, 3/6.

Lambert (*G. W., A. R. A.*), *The Art of.* Sydney Ure Smith and Leon Gellert, eds.

Pub. by Art in Australia, Ltd., 1924. 18 plates in colour, 75 plates in black and white. 600 copies. Pub. price, £3.3.0.

Lambert Memorial Number. Art in Australia, 3d Series, No. 33 (August, 1930). 8 plates in colour, 24 in black and white. Articles on Lambert by Julian Ashton, Arthur Streeton, W. B. Beattie, Norman Carter, Basil Burdett, Elioth Gruner, Hans Heysen, Arthur Adams, Harry Gullett, Daryl Lindsay, William Dalley, George Bell. Pub. price, 3/6.

Lambert (*G. W.*), *The Art and Life of.* By James MacDonald. Portrait in colour and 6 other illus., cr. 8vo, wrapper. Melbourne, n.d. Pub. price, 5/-.

Lindsay (*Norman*), *Pen Drawings.* 24 full-page plates. 500 signed copies. Folio, decorated boards. Sydney, Arthur McQuitty, 1924. Pub. price, £5.5.0.

Lindsay (*Norman*), *The Pen Drawings of.* Special number of Art in Australia. Sydney Ure Smith and Bertram Stevens, eds. 51 full-page plates, 4to, orig. wrapper. Sydney, 1918. Price, 21/-.

Lindsay (*Norman*), *The Pen Drawings of.* Sydney Ure Smith and Bertram Stevens, eds. Pub. by Angus & Robertson, Ltd., 1918. Ordinary edition. 51 plates, with article by Lionel Lindsay. Pub. price, 12/6. Out of print.

LINDSAY (LIONEL). 21 woodcuts, drawn, engraved, and printed by Lionel Lindsay. 30 signed copies on full vellum, decorated boards, vellum back. Privately printed on a hand press by Lionel Lindsay at the Meryen Press, Sydney, 1924. Pub. price, £10.10.0.

LINDSAY (LIONEL). A book of woodcuts; drawn on wood and engraved by Lionel Lindsay, with signed coloured woodcut front and 19 other plates. 35 numbered and signed copies, art boards. Art in Australia, Sydney, 1922. Pub. price, £7.10.0.

Lindsay (Lionel), Woodcuts by. Art in Australia, Ltd., 1922. 7½ x 10¾. 21 prints from the original woodcuts by the artist. 200 copies. Pub. price, £1.1.0.

Lindsay (Norman) Watercolour Book. Pub. by the Springwood Press, Sydney, 1939. 18 plates in colour. Biographical survey of the artist's life by Godfrey Blunden. Pub. price, £2.2.0.

Lindsay (Norman) Pen Drawings. Pub. by Art in Australia, Ltd., 1931. 64 plates. Article by Lionel Lindsay. Price, 5/–.

Lindsay (Norman) Number. Art in Australia, Ltd., 3d Series, No. 35 (December, 1930). 8 plates in colour, 35 in black and white. Articles by Kenneth Slessor. Pub. price, 3/6.

Lindsay (Lionel), The Art of. Art in Australia, 3d Series, No. 23 (March, 1928). 8 plates in colour, 60 plates in black and white. Articles by J. S. MacDonald and Harold Wright. Pub. price, 12/6.

Lindsay (Daryl) "Digger" Book. 450 numbered copies signed by the artist, with 14 plates, folio, boards. Sun Art Studios, Melbourne, 1919. Pub. price, 21/–.

Lindsay (Daryl) Number. Art in Australia, 3d Series, No. 39 (August, 1931). 8 plates in colour, 24 plates in black and white. Articles by Russell Grimwade and Basil Burdett. Pub. price, 3/6.

Long (Sydney). The etched work of Sydney Long, A.R.E. A complete catalogue of his etchings, edited by Dorothy Ellsmore Paul; 300 signed copies, with etched front, portrait and 27 plates, 4to, boards. The Attic Press, Sydney, 1928. Price, £3.3.0.

Longstaff (Sir John), The Art of. Art in Australia, 3d Series, No. 37 (April, 1931). 8 plates in colour, 28 plates in black and white. Articles by J. S. Mac-

Donald, Lionel Lindsay, Harold Herbert Pub. price, 5/6.

Low (David). *The Billy Book.* Hughes Abroad, with numerous cartoons by Low. 1st edition, orig. wrapper, enclosed in cloth slipcase. Sydney, 1918. Pub. price, 21/–.

Low, Caricatures by. Collected from the Sydney *Bulletin* and other sources. 250 copies, numbered and signed by the publisher, with portrait and numerous cartoons and 4 extra caricatures, in colour; folio, boards, canvas back. Sydney, 1915. Pub. price, £3.3.0.

Macquarie Book (The). Life and times of Governor Lachlan Macquarie; with portraits and plates (some in colour). Edition de luxe. 25 copies with engraver's proofs, 4to, decorated boards. Sydney, 1921. Pub. price, £2.2.0.

Macquarie Book (The). Pub. 1923. Edition de luxe. Art in Australia, No. 10, with the newly discovered portrait of Francis Greenway reproduced, and a Foreword giving particulars of the discovery of Greenway's portrait. The coloured plates are engraver's hand proofs. 25 copies. Pub. price, £3.3.0. Out of print.

MacNally (M. J.) and Harold Herbert, The Watercolours of. 7 x 8¾ ins. Pub. 1920. 12 plates in colour, and black and white. 600 copies. Pub. price, 10/6. Out of print.

McGrath (Eileen), The Work of. Special number of Art and Printing, designed and edited by G. Rayner Hoff, with 22 plates, 4to, wrapper. Sydney Technical College, 1931. Pub. price, 10/6.

McInnes (Beckwith), The Work of. With Biography by A. Colquhoun. Limited edition. 6 plates in colour and 13 in black and white, 4to, wrapper. Melbourne, n.d.

Martens (Conrad). The Man and His Art.

By Lionel Lindsay. 1st edition, with 32 colour plates, 12 sepia drawings, 16 pencil drawings, and 3 illus. in the text, 4to, board. Sydney, 1920. Pub. price, £2.2.0.

May (Phil) in Australia. With a chapter on his life and work by A. G. Stephens, and hundreds of humorous sketches and caricatures of prominent Australians in the artist's best manner. Edition de luxe. 25 copies with additional engravings bound ("Some Notorious People in Australia") and 1 additional loose plate (should be 2), folio, buckram. Sydney, 1904. Price, £3.10.0.

Meldrum (Max). His Art and Views. Colin Colahan, ed. 45 illus. 150 copies, signed; 4to, half suede. Melbourne, n.d. Pub. price, 21/–.

Minns (B. E.) Number. Art in Australia, 3d Series, No. 47 (December, 1932). 6 plates in colour, 18 plates in black and white. Articles by Julian Ashton and M. J. MacNally. Pub. price, 3/6.

Moore's (John D.) Watercolours. Art in Australia, 3d Series, No. 62 (October, 1933). 6 plates in colour, 16 plates in black and white. Articles by Norman Carter and Basil Burdett. Pub. price, 3/6.

MOORE (WILLIAM). *The Story of Australian Art.* From the earliest known art of the Continent to the art of today. With a Foreword by Julian Ashton. 248 illus., 2 vols., roy. 8vo. Sydney, 1934. Pub. price, £2.10.0.

Nicholas (Hilda Rix), The Art of. 16 plates (7 in colour), sm. 4to, wrapper. 1919. Pub. price, 3/6.

Old Colonial By-Ways. By CHARLES H. BERTIE; illustrations by Sydney Ure Smith. Pub. by Art in Australia, Ltd. 7 plates in colour, 48 plates in black and white. Pub. price, 12/6.

Preston (Margaret) Number. Art in Australia. Edition de luxe. 25 copies. Original coloured woodcut by Margaret Preston, designed for this book and the block since destroyed; together with 49 other plates, of which 22 are in colour. sm. 4to, boards. Sydney, 1927. 30/–.

Preston (Margaret) Number. Art in Australia, 3d Series, No. 22 (December, 1927). 22 plates in colour, 28 plates in black and white. Articles by A. Radcliffe Brown, Thea Proctor, and Margaret Preston. Pub. price, 12/6.

Proctor (Thea) Number. Art in Australia, 3d Series, No. 43 (April, 1932). 4 plates in colour, 16 plates in black and white. Articles by Ethel Anderson and Basil Burdett. Pub. price, 3/9.

Ramsay (Hugh), The Art of. 6 plates in colour, 7 in black and white. sm. 4to, boards. Melbourne, n.d. Pub. price, 5/–.

Shirlow (John) Etchings. With Introduction by Sydney Ure Smith. 24 sepia-toned etchings, cr. 8vo, wrapper. Sydney, 1917. 2/6.

Society of Artists' Pictures. Special number of Art in Australia. Sydney Ure Smith and Bertram Stevens, eds. Pub. by Angus & Robertson, Ltd., 1920. An illustrated record of The Society of Artists' Annual Exhibition, 1919. 20 plates in colour, 30 in black and white. Pub. price, 12/6. Out of print.

The Society of Artists' Exhibition, 1923. Art in Australia, Ltd. 52 plates in colour, and in black and white, illustrating the Society of Artists' Annual Exhibition. Pub. price, £1.1.0.

Streeton (Arthur), The Art of. Sydney Ure Smith and Bertram Stevens, eds. Pub. by Angus & Robertson, Ltd., 1919. 8¾ x 10¼ ins. 30 plates in colour, and 20 in black and white. Articles by Lionel

Lindsay and P. G. Konody. 1,000 copies. Pub. price, £2.2.0. Out of print.

Streeton (Arthur) Number. Art in Australia, 3d Series, No. 40 (October, 1931). 8 plates in colour, 25 plates in black and white. Articles by Lionel Lindsay and J. S. MacDonald. Pub. price, 3/9.

Smith (Sydney Ure), The Etchings of. Published uniform with the MacNally, Herbert Book. A revised catalogue of etchings with descriptive notes, including reproductions. Pub. price, 10/6.

Smith (Sydney Ure) and Lionel Lindsay: Windsor, N.S.W. Pub. 1921. 8 orig. etchings and one woodblock by Lionel Lindsay and Sydney Ure Smith. With article by J. H. M. Abbott printed on hand press, handset type. 16 copies. 10¾ x 15. Pub. price, 20 guineas. Out of print.

Smith (Sydney Ure), A Catalogue of the Etchings of. 10¼ x 7¾. Edition de luxe, printed on a hand press on handmade paper, with 1 orig. etching and 12 reproductions. Complete list of plates with descriptive notes. Introduction by Bertram Stevens. 50 copies, numbered and signed. Pub. price, £3.3.0. Out of print.

Smith (Sydney Ure), Etchings of. 35 copies, with an orig. etching, and 78 plates; small folio, one of 2 copies specially bound in full dark-blue crushed morocco, with gilt decoration, by Wal Taylor. Sydney, 1921. Price, £5.5.0.

Smith (Sydney Ure), The Etchings of. 300 copies. 78 plates, 8vo, wrapper. Sydney, 1920. Pub. price, 15/–.

Smith (Sydney Ure), Relics of Old Colonial Days. A book of 21 drawings, 500 signed copies, wrapper, 4to. Sydney, 1914. Pub. price, 10/6.

Streeton (Arthur), The Catalogue. Pub. by the artist, Melbourne, 1935. 26 plates in colour, 18 in black and white. Contains complete catalogue of artist's work.

Tasmanian Number. Art in Australia, 3d Series, No. 30 (December, 1929). 5 plates in colour, 47 in black and white. Article by Clive Lord. Pub. price, 12/6.

Wilson (Hardy). The Cowpasture Road. Written and illustrated by Hardy Wilson. Art in Australia, Ltd., 1920. A fantasy on the early days in New South Wales; 12 plates in colour, and black and white. 600 copies. Pub. price, £2.2.0. Out of print.

Wilson (Hardy). The Cowpasture Road. 11 plates (7 in colour) and a map of the Cowpasture Road. 25 copies, of which 10 are for sale in Australia, with engraver's proofs of the plates, 4to, vellum. Sydney, 1920. Pub. price, £7.10.0.

Wilson (Hardy). Early Grecian and Chinese Architecture. 50 plates, 4 pencil drawings by Hardy Wilson with article by the author (1937). 100 copies. Pub. by the author, 92 Queen St., Melbourne. Pub. price, £6.6.0.

Wilson (Hardy). Old Colonial Architecture in New South Wales and Tasmania. 50 full-page plates from pencil drawings by the author. 1,000 copies. Pub. by the author, Union House, Sydney, 1924. Price, £10.10.0.

Withers (Walter), The Life and Art of. Australian Art Book Series. Plates, cr. 8vo, wrapper. Melbourne, n.d. Pub. price, 1/6.

Young (Blamire), The Art of. Sydney Ure Smith and Bertram Stevens, eds. Pub. by Angus & Robertson, Ltd., 1921. Uniform with Streeton and Heysen Books. 36 plates in colour. Articles by James F. Bruce. Pub. price, £2.2.0. Out of print.

Nos. 3 and 4. ABORIGINAL BARK DRAWINGS. The drawings are on sheets of eucalyptus bark; the medium used is red or yellow ochre, white clay and charcoal. They have no religious or ceremonial significance. A peculiar feature is that internal structures, such as the backbone and digestive tract, are often indicated.

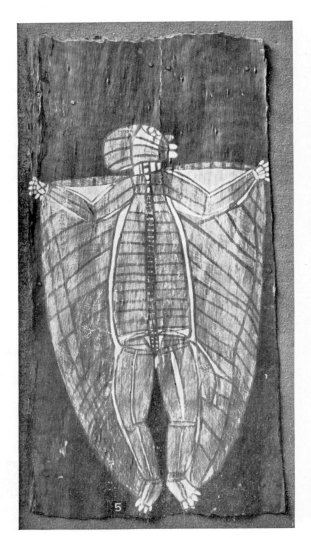 

Nos. 6 and 11. ABORIGINAL BARK DRAWINGS. The painting is
done with the chewed and frayed end of a reed and by blowing masticated
pigment over hands and feet.

No. 12. PEN DRAWING BY VICTORIAN ABORIGINES. White man's materials were here used. While clearly primitive, they show a fairly advanced conception of design and action.

No. 15. SYDNEY ABOUT 1815, artist unknown. This portrays the town when it was 27 years old, and during the governorship of Lachlan Macquarie, one of the outstanding early officials. He found it a place of mean buildings and narrow, sordid streets; he left it clean and laid out on a dignified and appropriate plan. Macquarie also did much to improve the conditions of the convicts and ex-convicts.

No. 16. SYDNEY FROM THE WEST SIDE OF THE COVE, ABOUT 1809, by John Eyre. This painting, one of a set of four, shows the town just after the rebellion against Governor Bligh, formerly the victim of the *Bounty* mutiny. Bligh was at this time a prisoner in the town, and the government was under the control of officers in the New South Wales Corps. The building just below the windmill was Government House.

No. 18. SUBSCRIPTION BALL, BALLARAT, 1854, by Samuel Thomas Gill. At this time the Ballarat goldfields had been operated for three years. A population of 20,000 had assembled, whose robust and boisterous prosperity is here indicated. The banner on the musicians' gallery has historical significance, as showing an early impulse toward federation of the then entirely separate colonies. The kangaroo and emu, first appearing on flags in 1805, were incorporated in the arms of the Commonwealth in 1908.

No. 21. GOLD DIGGERS, ARARAT, 1854, by J. Roper. The Australian Gold Rush began in 1851, and played the same sort of part in developing the country, especially Victoria, as the almost contemporary California rush. Victoria's population increased from 77,000 to 236,000 in three years. Some of these goldfields were among the richest alluvial deposits ever discovered. In these early camps justice was administered by a Committee of Safety.

No. 22. H.M.S. *MERMAID* WATERING, by Philip Parker King. While engaged on a survey of the coast of western Australia, 1818–22, a watering party from the cutter *Mermaid* was attacked by natives, as here shown. The incident occurred at Goulbourn Island.

No. 24. MY HARVEST HOME, by John Glover. This scene well represents the softness and fertility of the Tasmanian landscape, which offers a striking contrast to the grim grandeur of most of Australia.

No. 25. PORTRAIT OF MRS. WILSON, by Thomas Griffiths Waine-wright. This highly sophisticated drawing was the work of one of the most shameless murderers that ever escaped the gallows.

No. 27. STILL LIFE, FRUIT AND FLOWERS, by William Barlow
Gould. After his release, this artist often exchanged these refined products
for drink, and at one time nearly every public house in Hobart possessed
one or more of them.

No. 31. A SOLITARY RAMBLE, by Julian Ashton, C.B.E. This picture shows the full measure of social and artistic development attained in Australia in the 'eighties.

No. 34. DOWN ON HIS LUCK, by Frederick McCubbin. This represents a swaggie, or sundowner—the Australian equivalent of a hobo. When on the track a swaggie says he is "waltzing Matilda," or "on the wallaby." The swaggie of the picture has had the misfortune to overturn his pot and lose his prospect of a cup of tea. Still familiar in the Australian bush, the swaggie is gradually being pushed westward.

No. 35. SHEARING THE RAMS, by Tom Roberts. This important pictorial record of a leading Australian industry was painted at Brocklesby, N.S.W., in the 'eighties, and took about eight months to complete. A first-class shearer would average 200 sheep a day. The small boy in the center background was called the "tar boy"; it was his duty to smear on a dab of tar when a sheep was nicked.

No. 36. BAILED UP, by Tom Roberts. This represents a holdup in the bushranging days. The bushrangers mostly came from small farms, tempted by the gold which was being transported across country to the coast. The VR under the box indicates that this vehicle is a mail coach. The quietness of the scene is said to be wholly typical of the manner in which the act was performed. Begun in 1898, this picture was largely re-painted 30 years later.

No. 40. RAT'S CASTLE, by Blamire Young. Both realistic and romantic, this water colour exhibits a twentieth-century viewpoint through which the influence of the great English romantic water-colourists, such as J. S. Cotman, is clearly visible.

No. 45. PASSING SHOWERS, by Sir Arthur Streeton. "Plein air" painting, Australian version, at its height.

No. 49. SERGEANT OF THE AUSTRALIAN LIGHT HORSE, GALLIPOLI, by George Washington Lambert, A.R.A. Lambert, while official artist with the Australian Imperial Forces, 1914–18, acquired a thorough knowledge of all phases of life in a cavalry regiment. This typically lean, rangy trooper, with his plume of emu feathers, represents a method of warfare now almost as far from us as the feats of Murat and J. E. B. Stuart.

No. 50. WEIGHING THE FLEECE, by G. W. Lambert, A.R.A.
Merino sheep were imported from Spain as early as 1794; since then much
ingenuity has been displayed by breeders in selecting strains best suited
to the Australian vegetation and climate. One of the most serviceable has
been found to be the Vermont strain, developed subsequently to David
Humphreys' original importation of merinos to the U.S.A., soon after
1800. The average weight of such a fleece as here shown would be 25
pounds, the average price, 14d. per pound. Prize rams have brought
prices up to 5,000 guineas.

No. 62. LAND OF ORATUNGA, by Hans Heysen. These bold ridges of the Flinders Range in Central Australia have rock colors of pink, orange and red, but an annual rainfall of only five inches makes the vegetation extremely sparse.

No. 68. "SUMMERLEES," SUTTON FOREST, by Charles Lloyd Jones. Trained as an artist, Jones is now head of the largest department store in Australia. He still paints, exhibits regularly in the principal shows, and is represented in many national collections. He was one of the founders, with Sydney Ure Smith, of *Art in Australia* and is now Chairman of Directors of *Australia, National Journal*.

No. 72. TIMBER GETTERS, by J. J. Hilder. In the early days wasteful cutting destroyed the Australian forests much as in the United States. Recently the Government has laid down regulations and spent much money and effort on reforestation. The chief tree of commerce is the eucalyptus, of which there are more than four hundred varieties.

No. 75. MT. TENNANT, CANBERRA, by Elioth Gruner. The Capital
Territory of the Australian Commonwealth was discovered and settled in
the 1820's. Lying high on the southern plateau of New South Wales, it
consists mostly of fine pasture land. In the early days it was infested with
bushrangers, mostly at that time ex-convicts turned bandit. Mt. Tennant
was named after one of these, who was hanged in 1828.

No. 77. ABORIGINAL STILL LIFE, by Margaret Preston. This artist is a great admirer of aboriginal arts and crafts, not only for their own value but as the foundation of an original and national art. Here she has happily combined native shields with the stiff leaves and cones of the banksia tree.

No. 83. ROMANTIC LANDSCAPE, by Roland Wakelin. Post-impressionist influence became important in Australia shortly after the last war, and Wakelin is a leading exponent of the modern group. This view shows a reach of Sydney Harbour, whose natural beauties are now protected by zoning.

No. 88. KURRAJONG FARM, by John D. Moore. The work of this successful architect-artist, who paints both in oils and water colours, shows free and powerful handling and strong modern French influence.

No. 92. CHURCH ON THE HILL, by John Roy Eldershaw. The subject of this picture is St. Johns, Richmond, Tasmania, the oldest extant Catholic church in Australia. It was opened in 1837 as the result of the efforts of a priest named Polding, the then Apostolic Vicar of New South Wales.

No. 97. FLOWERS IN SUNLIGHT, by Adrian Feint. This vigorous
work is from the hand of the leading Australian designer of bookplates.

No. 101. CABBAGE GUMS AND CYPRESS PINES, by Kenneth MacQueen. "Gum" in Australia is the common term for eucalyptus. The name "cabbage" derives from the shape of the foliage masses. The cypress pine is valuable not only for its timber but for its rosin and its bark, which yields tannin. These trees may have been painted on MacQueen's own Queensland farm.

No. 110. BOY AT THE BASIN, by William Dobell. The restrained
humanism, somewhat reminiscent of Daumier, of Dobell's earlier work
has passed into the more riotous phase shown in *The Tattooed Woman*,
No. 111.

No. 113. SPRING AT ARALUEN, by Eileen Crow. Even under the hand of modernism the Tasmanian landscape retains its pastoral and idyllic character.

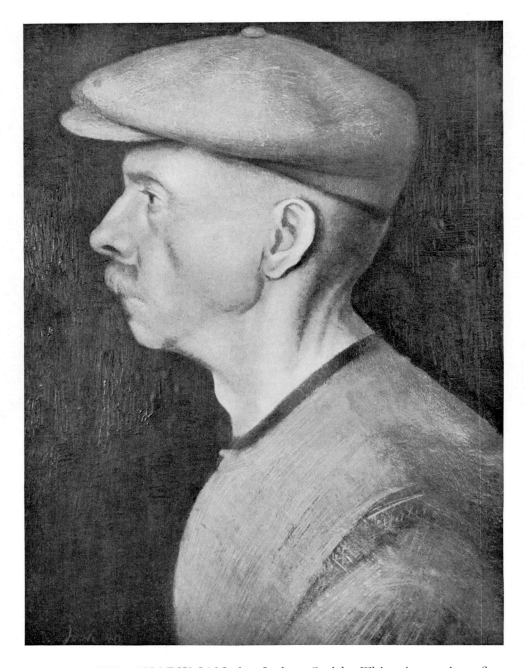

No. 114. THE WORKMAN, by Joshua Smith. This picture is a fine example of the influence of post-impressionism on an ineradicably British personality. The chief net result is simplicity and sincerity.

No. 117. DESIGN FOR AN ABORIGINAL BALLET, NO. 1, by William Constable. This namesake of a great Englishman has recently designed decors and costumes for four Russian ballets, one classical Greek play, seven modern dramas, four Shakespearian plays and a musical comedy.

No. 119b. THE RABBITER AND HIS FAMILY, by George Russell
Drysdale. The rabbiter and his motley pack of dogs is a familiar figure in a
country where the rabbit is a national pest.

No. 125. THE DIPLOMATS, by Peter Purves Smith. In addition to a finely conceived pattern, this picture shows the social and international consciousness frequent among the younger artists in all countries.

No. 134. ABORIGINAL HEAD (bronze), by Lyndon Dadswell. Present-day Australians show a lively interest in all phases of aboriginal life, which, owing to the unsuitability of much of the country to white man's exploitation, still survives in considerable extent and purity.

No. 120. PORT PHILLIP BAY, by Lina Bryans. This vigorous canvas, largely painted with the knife, retains a strong feeling of Australian landscape.

No. 123. EARLY COLONIAL ARCHITECTURE, by Elaine Haxton. A scene in Elizabeth Bay Crescent, Sydney, one of the oldest parts of the city. Jigsaw, cast iron and mansard roofs were as popular in Australia during mid-19th century days as in the United States. In view of the fact that this picture was painted after an extensive stay in the U.S.A., it may be conjectured that the influence of Charles Burchfield is discernible.